WHAT ON EARTH IS GOD DOING?

Satan's Conflict With God

Updated & Revised

WHAT ON EARTH IS GOD DOING?

SATAN'S CONFLICT WITH GOD

RENALD E. SHOWERS

Updated & Revised

The Friends of Israel Gospel Ministry, Inc.
P. O. Box 908, Bellmawr, NJ 08099

WHAT ON EARTH IS GOD DOING? (Updated and Revised)
Renald E. Showers

Originally published by Loizeaux Brothers, Inc. (Copyright © 1973) with the original ISBN 0-87213-784-8 and Library of Congress Catalog Card Number 73:81551

Copyright © 2003 by The Friends of Israel Gospel Ministry, Inc. Bellmawr, NJ 08099

3rd Printing by The Friends of Israel 2005

Library of Congress Number: 2002116562
ISBN: 0-915540-80-0

Cover by Gariel Graphics, Woodbury, NJ.

Visit our Web site at www.foi.org.

This book is dedicated to
my wife, Eleanor,
and my daughters, Renee and Marbeth,
who have contributed so much
to my life and ministry.

CONTENTS

INTRODUCTION

SATAN WORSHIP, WITCHCRAFT, SPIRITISM, and astrology—the present revival of the occult is only one phase of the continuing war of the ages between God and Satan. Apart from a knowledge of this war it is impossible to understand what life is all about, and the only way to learn about this conflict is to study the philosophy of history presented by the Bible.

For centuries mankind has been wrestling with three major questions: Where have we come from? Why are we here? Where are we going? Numerous attempts have been made to answer these questions. Each attempt could be called a philosophy of life or history.

The Bible deals with these three questions; therefore, there is a biblical philosophy of history. The purpose of this study is to attempt to trace the Bible's philosophy of history from eternity past to eternity future. In making this attempt it is important to call to the reader's attention several factors. First, time and space will not permit this study to deal with most historical events related in the Bible or in extra-Biblical sources. The intention is to demonstrate God's purpose for history by giving a bird's-eye view of events.

Secondly, statements will be made to the effect that God or Satan did certain things. Such statements are not meant to imply that in every instance God or Satan was the person actually performing the action. Occasionally God and Satan do intervene directly in history, but more frequently they carry out their purposes through intermediate agents. They both prompt and use the actions of humans, nations, and angels for their own purposes.

Thirdly, the Bible records selected historic events only to the end of the first century A.D. It also deals prophetically with future events. However, it does not cover specific events that have transpired from the end of the first century to the present. In spite of this last factor, the Bible does present its philosophy of history in such a way as to provide a framework by which events of the present dispensation can be interpreted. For this reason the scope of this study will include selected events from the end of the first century to the present.

1

THE SETTING FOR THE CONFLICT

From Eternity Past Through Creation

THE BIBLE'S PHILOSOPHY OF HISTORY begins with the eternal, personal God who existed as three distinct Persons: Father, Son, and Spirit. Prior to creation nothing else existed but God.

In eternity past God determined to have a kingdom over which He could rule as sovereign King (1 Tim. 1:17). Since it is impossible to have a kingdom without subjects, and since nothing else existed to serve Him, God created the subjects over which He was to rule.

The personal, created subjects were of two major kinds. First, God created angelic subjects. These angels were spirit beings, not possessing bodies of flesh and bone (Mt. 22:30; Heb. 1:13–14), but they did possess intellect (2 Sam. 14:20) and the ability to communicate (Gen. 19:1–2). They were more powerful than the other kind of created beings (2 Pet. 2:11). Although made to dwell in the heavens, they were given access to earth after its creation (Gen. 19:1; Mt. 24:36). Certain angels were made superior in intelligence, power, and authority over others (Dan. 10:13; Eph. 1:21; Col. 1:16). The Bible does not reveal exactly how many angels God created, but it does mention one hundred million plus thousands of thousands more (Dan. 7:10; Heb. 12:22; Rev. 5:11).

The second major kind of personal subject created for God's kingdom was the human being. Inasmuch as God had created the earth to be part of His domain, He intended to have on it a kind of subject that would administer His rule over everything else on the planet. Just as some kings divide their kingdoms into provinces, place a subject as governor over each province, and hold each governor responsible to administer his province well on behalf of the king, so God created man, placed him as governor over the earth, and held him responsible to administer the earth well on behalf of God (Gen. 1:26, 28; Ps. 8:3–9). In other words, God intended the government of the earth to be a theocracy. According to *The Oxford English Dictionary*, a theocracy is

A form of government in which God (or a deity) is recognized as the king or immediate ruler, and his laws are taken as the statute-book of the kingdom, these laws usually being administered by . . . a representative or representatives as his ministers and agents.[1]

Man had to be specially equipped in order to govern the earth for God. It was essential that he be able to understand his earthly, physical province; therefore, God formed for him a physical body from the dust of the earth (Gen. 2:7). It also was necessary that he be able to receive and understand God's directions; therefore, God created man in His own image (Gen. 1:26–28) as a personal being possessing intellect and the ability to communicate.

With the creation of man, God's work of bringing His kingdom into existence was completed. The universal kingdom of God was a reality, and everything in it was very good by God's perfect standard of evaluation (Gen. 1:31).

From the Fall of Angels
Through the Promise of the Redeemer

Satan's Rebellion

After creation was completed, one of the highest angels became so proud of his great intelligence and powers that he deceived himself into thinking that he could overthrow the sovereign rule of God (Isa. 14:12–14; Ezek. 28:11–17; 1 Tim. 3:6). He hoped to make himself the king of the universe by establishing a kingdom of his own that would war against and destroy God's kingdom. Because of this angel's rebellion against God, his name was changed to Satan, which means "adversary."[2] He had become the great revolutionary, the enemy of God and every member of God's kingdom (Mt. 13:25, 28, 39; Lk. 10:18–19).

At this point it is important to note something about Satan. In spite of his proud plans, he will never be more than a creature of God's. In this respect the biblical philosophy of history differs radically from those religious and philosophical systems that picture a struggle between two equal gods, one good and one evil. According to the Bible, there can be no doubt about God, the Creator, defeating Satan, the creature. In fact, God could have crushed Satan's rebellion as soon as it began, but in His sovereign will He chose not to do so. The reason for this choice will be seen later.

The Rebellion of Other Angels

In order to establish his kingdom, Satan had to obtain subjects over which to rule. As a creature he lacked ability to create beings. For him the only possible way to obtain subjects was by persuading God's other creatures to join him in his rebellion. If his kingdom were to rule over both heavenly and earthly spheres, he had to persuade both angels and humans to join him.

A sizeable number of angels did join Satan's rebellion and place themselves under his rule. There are several biblical references to Satan "and his angels" (Mt. 25:41; Rev. 12:7). As a result of this angelic decision, Satan became the prince of angels (Mt. 12:24–26), the ruler of the authority of the air (Eph. 2:2). Satan organized his angels in several ranks so that they could carry on the work of his kingdom efficiently (Eph. 6:11).

Although a sizeable number of angels transferred their allegiance from the kingdom of God to the kingdom of Satan, a huge host of angels chose to remain faithful to God. These are called the "holy" and "elect" angels (Mk. 8:38; 1 Tim. 5:21). God remained the Lord of these hosts (Isa. 54:5; Jer. 31:35). Thus God's kingdom continued to possess a multitude of angelic subjects within it.

Man's Rebellion

In a very subtle way Satan entered man's perfect earthly environment and tempted man to disobey a specific command of God. The bait that Satan used was the notion that, if man would disobey, he would become as God (Gen. 3:1–5). In other words, he was telling man that he could be his own sovereign, that he could rule his own life, if only he would rebel. In spite of God's warning, man decided to disobey the directive of his divine King. Thus the governor of the earthly province of the kingdom of God joined the rebellion against God.

The Consequences of Man's Rebellion

Several tragic consequences resulted from man's rebellion. First, man died spiritually at the moment of his disobedience (Gen. 2:16–17). This does not mean that the immaterial part of man passed out of existence. Instead, it means that man suffered a drastic change in his nature. God had created man with a disposition that was favorable toward God and that affected the rest of man's nature. As a result, man fellowshipped with and served God in a proper way. When man rebelled, he lost his favorable disposition toward God and became confirmed in a disposition of enmity against God (Rom. 8:7). Man's whole being became so fully controlled by this disposition of enmity that his entire nature suffered a perversion called total depravity. As a result of this depravity, man's relationship to God, the Source of life, was broken.

Second, eventually man died physically. When man rebelled, a process of decay began operating in his body. It made him subject to disease, deformity, and death (Gen. 3:19; 5:5; Rom. 5:12; 6:23; Heb. 9:27). In addition to death by decay, man became subject to death by hazards, accidents, and violence (Gen. 4:8; 9:5–6; Lk. 13:4). Because of his rebellion, man was denied access to a source that would cause him to live forever (Gen. 3:22–24).

Third, man's ability to exercise dominion over the earth was changed. He lost ability to govern some things (Heb. 2:5–8). The ability that he did retain became perverted. As a result, he became doomed to abuse the earth. Because of his attitude of enmity against God, man began to exercise his dominion in a manner contrary to what God had intended.

Fourth, because man was the governor of the earthly province of God's kingdom, his rebellion brought tragedy to his domain. A province of a kingdom often suffers as a result of its governor's choice to rebel against the king. In man's domain, the productive level of the soil was reduced greatly (Gen. 3:17), and for the first time the soil brought forth thorns and thistles (Gen. 3:18). Animal nature changed drastically from a tame, noncarnivorous state (Gen. 1:30) to a wild, carnivorous state. Romans 8:19–22 indicates that all of God's earthly creation became subject to vanity and corruption because of man's rebellion. As a result, it continues to groan and travail in pain to the present day. Through his own sin man lost his perfect environment.

Fifth, man was transferred from membership in the kingdom of God to membership in the kingdom of Satan. This consequence had a tragic effect upon the whole human race. Because the original parents of the race chose to rebel against God, and because humans reproduce after their kind, every human (except Christ) born in the world is born with a disposition of enmity against God. Thus every human is born spiritually dead and a member of Satan's kingdom (Eph. 2:1). Unless he accepts God's way of salvation (to be discussed later), each human continues through life to be energized by Satan and to live his life according to Satan's ways (Eph. 2:2); to be blinded to the truth by Satan (2 Cor. 4:4); to be deceived by Satan into believing that error is truth (2 Cor. 11:14–15); to be in spiritual darkness and to be held in Satan's power (Acts 26:17–18); to be a child of Satan (Mt. 13:37–39; Jn. 8:44; 1 Jn. 3:8, 10); and to head for the same place of judgment as Satan (Mt. 13:40–42; 25:41; Rev. 20:10, 15). Second Corinthians 6:14–15 indicates that every unsaved person belongs to Satan and his kingdom of darkness. Satan uses unsaved people to do some of the work of his kingdom (Job 1:9–15, 17; Lk. 22:3–6; Jn. 8:37, 40, 44, 59; 2 Th. 2:9; 1 Jn. 3:12).

Sixth, because Adam, the governor of the earthly province of God's universal kingdom, had defected from God, the theocracy was lost and Satan was able to usurp the rule of the world system away from God. The earth's government changed from a theocracy to a satanocracy. For this reason Christ called Satan "the prince of this world" (Jn. 12:31; 14:30; 16:11); Satan had authority to offer all the kingdoms of the world to Christ (Lk. 4:5–6); some of Satan's angels are called "the world-rulers of this darkness" (Eph. 6:12, literal translation of Greek text); "the whole world lies in the evil one" (1 Jn. 5:19, literal translation of Greek text); and Satan dominates the present age of the world so completely that the apostle Paul called him "the god of this age" (2 Cor. 4:4, literal translation of Greek text).

These tragic consequences reveal that man had been duped by Satan into believing a lie (Jn. 8:44). Instead of bringing man freedom, rebellion against God's authority brought man slavery to a sinful disposition (Rom. 6:6, 16–23), to death (Rom. 5:12; Heb. 9:27), and to the continual fear of death throughout life (Heb. 2:15). Instead of becoming his own sovereign, man had been brought under the dominion of a new king. His original King was a loving, benevolent Ruler who offered man life, peace, happiness, and fulfillment in return for willing obedience. But his new king was a hard, selfish taskmaster who offered man death, sickness, conflict, grief, and frustration in return for service to him. Instead of improving himself by rebellion against God, man had prevented himself from obtaining the fullness of his original potential. He had debased himself and lost much of his intended dignity (Rom. 1:18–32).

Man's rebellion confirmed him so strongly in his tragic predicament that he was rendered totally incapable of rescuing himself from it. Quite frequently his invention of ingenious devices or programs to improve his lot would boomerang and bring new problems not previously anticipated. Nothing short of supernatural, divine intervention would be able to save man from the predicament he had brought upon himself by his own choice (Isa. 43:11).

With the fall of man the personnel of Satan's kingdom was complete. He had succeeded in transferring many of God's angels and all of God's humans into his domain. In the process he had brought the world system under his rule. In this he appeared to be enjoying initial success in his challenge of God's sovereign rule.

The Purpose of History

Now there were two opposing kingdoms in existence. The kingdom of Satan had attacked the kingdom of God with the goal of destroying it. If God were to remain sovereign, He must crush Satan and his kingdom. Thus the stage was set for a fantastic conflict—the conflict of the ages. This conflict would be waged both in the heavens and on the earth (Rev. 12:7, 13, 17; Eph. 6:10–12). Since the Bible is God's written revelation to *man*, it deals primarily with the earthly phase of the conflict.

This conflict of the ages provides the key for unlocking the mystery of the ultimate purpose of history. Both God and Satan have a purpose for history; but since God is God, and Satan is only a creature, God's purpose is the ultimate one. Satan's purpose for history is to make himself the only sovereign king of the universe by establishing his kingdom as the only permanent one of the heavens, the earth, and all that is in them. When first set up, his kingdom was not permanently established as an everlasting one. It could become such only if Satan could crush God and His kingdom. This he has been attempting since his own rebellion began, and the attempt will continue almost to the end of this present world's history.

God's purpose for history is to glorify Himself by demonstrating the fact that He alone is the sovereign God of the universe. Inasmuch as God's purpose for history is the ultimate one, it is correct to conclude that *the ultimate purpose for history is for God to glorify Himself by demonstrating His sovereignty.*

In order to demonstrate His sovereignty during history, God must restore the present earth to the basic original condition it enjoyed before man's rebellion. Old Testament prophets received revelation to the effect that He would do just that (Acts 3:21). It is important to note that the restoration must take place on this present earth, not the new earth to be created by God for eternity future (Rev. 21:1). Should God permit the present earth to pass away at the end of history without restoring it to its original conditions, it would appear that He was incapable of overcoming the devastating work of Satan and his kingdom. Thus there would be no demonstration of divine sovereignty during history.

In order to restore the present earth to its original conditions, God must reverse during history all the tragic consequences of man's rebellion. First, He must make humans spiritually alive again. This would involve His giving to people a new, confirmed disposition of love and obedience toward God and the indwelling Holy Spirit to control the whole of a person's nature in accordance with God's will.

Second, God must abolish physical death. This would involve ending and reversing decay in man's body; abolishing disease, deformity, hazards, accidents, and violence; and resurrecting the bodies of those already dead.

Third, God must cause man to govern the present earth in the manner that He intended originally. This would involve a restoration of the governing ability man lost, a correction of the ability he retained in perverted form, and an end of man's abuse of the earth.

Fourth, God must restore the perfect environment that man enjoyed before the fall. This would involve changing the soil to its original, fertile condition; restoring animal nature to its state of being tame and noncarnivorous; and removing the vanity and corruption to which all earthly creation has been subject since man rebelled.

Fifth, God must transfer human beings from membership in Satan's kingdom to membership in the kingdom of God by causing these humans to experience a new, spiritual birth.

Sixth, God must crush His enemy, Satan, rid the earth of him and his kingdom, and then reestablish His theocratic kingdom on this present earth. This means that the future Millennium is absolutely essential for God to accomplish His purpose for history. If that millennial restoration of God's theocracy does not take place before the history of this present earth ends, then God ends up being defeated by His enemy, Satan, within the scope of this present earth's history.

The reversal of the consequences of man's sin could be called God's program of redemption.

The First Promise of the Coming Redeemer

In light of the necessity for God to crush Satan and his kingdom in order to demonstrate divine sovereignty, it is interesting to note that no sooner had Satan usurped the world system for his kingdom than God delivered a prophecy concerning Satan's doom (Gen. 3:14–15). In this prophecy God addressed Satan in the subtle form that he had taken to tempt man. God forewarned Satan that eventually a man born of woman would deliver a devastating blow to him. Later Scripture revealed that this prophecy was God's initial way of promising that a Redeemer would be born in the world and that this Redeemer would do the work necessary to crush Satan's kingdom and work. In other words, the Redeemer was to be God's Counterrevolutionary who would make possible the defeat of the great revolutionary. The Redeemer, then, was to be the key to the fulfillment of God's purpose for history.

In order for God to reverse the consequences of man's sin, it was necessary to get rid of the cause of the consequences. This meant getting rid of human sin. Later Scripture revealed that only the payment of an adequate penalty to divine justice could remove man's sin. It also revealed that death was the only adequate penalty (Rom. 5:12; 6:23). Because of this, in the Genesis 3:15 prophecy God also foretold that, while the Redeemer would crush Satan, Satan would bruise Him. This was God's way of saying that, as a result of Satan's work, the promised Redeemer would suffer death in order to defeat Satan. Later Scripture revealed that through His death the Redeemer would pay the penalty for man's sin, thereby causing the removal of sin (Isa. 53:4–6,10—12; Jn. 1:29) and making it possible for God to reverse the consequences of man's rebellion.

The Strategy of the Conflict

Genesis 3:15 made it evident that God intended the Redeemer to be the heart of His strategy in the war against Satan. The Redeemer, however, would not be the only person to serve the kingdom of God in the conflict. The holy, elect angels would fight against the forces of Satan (Dan. 10:20; Rev. 12:7). Through the redemptive work of the Redeemer, God would save people out of Satan's kingdom and make them members of His own kingdom (Gal. 1:4; Col. 1:13). These redeemed humans would remain in the world for the rest of their lives to act as representatives of the kingdom of God in the world system dominated by Satan. Although they would live in Satan's world system, they would not belong to it (Jn. 17:14–18). They would be strangers and pilgrims in the world with their citizenship in heaven (Eph. 2:19; Phil. 3:20; Heb. 11:13; 1 Pet. 1:17).

Occasionally God also would use nations and even unsaved people to serve His purposes (Isa. 10:5–6; Isa. 44:28—45:5; Jer. 25:9). Thus, although God's kingdom would not exist in a worldwide theocratic form during certain periods of history, it would be represented and working in the world during every period of history. This continuing function of the universal kingdom of God in the world system dominated by Satan helps to explain the continuing presence of good alongside of evil in the world (Mt. 13:24–30, 36–43).

Since the coming and work of the Redeemer would be the key to God's strategy, the key to Satan's strategy would be the preventing of the Redeemer's coming and work. In addition, Satan would war against the holy angels and redeemed humans who would represent God's kingdom in the world (Dan. 10:13, 20–21; Eph. 6:11, 16). He would use his fallen angels, the human members of his kingdom, nations, and occasionally even humans from God's kingdom to do his work (Job 1:9–15, 17; Dan. 10:13, 20–21; Mt. 16:21–23; Lk. 22:3; Acts 5:1–3; Eph. 6:12; 2 Th. 2:9).

A study of the Scriptures indicates that Satan intended to use interchangeably two different lines of attack: (1) try to destroy the members of God's kingdom and (2) try to pervert the witness of God's kingdom with apostasy in belief or practice. Both tactics will be observed repeatedly as the drama of the conflict unfolds.

2

THE CONFLICT
FROM THE FIRST HUMAN BIRTH
THROUGH THE WILDERNESS WANDERINGS

The First Birth and Murder

SATAN WAS PRESENT IN EDEN TO hear God's first promise of the coming Redeemer. He realized that it would be fatal for him and his cause if the Redeemer were to come. Thus Satan's primary goal throughout Old Testament history became the prevention of the Redeemer's coming.

Sometime after Adam and Eve gave birth to Cain and Abel, it became evident that one son was godly in attitude and that the other was ungodly. Evidently Abel's godly attitude convinced Satan that Abel was either the Redeemer or the one through whose line of descent the Redeemer would come. Thus it became imperative to Satan to get rid of Abel. Inasmuch as Cain already was controlled by a rebellious, angry attitude, it didn't take much to prompt him to kill his brother (Gen. 4:1–8). That Satan was involved in Cain's slaying of his brother was made evident in 1 John 3:10–12. Because of Satan's involvement Christ stated that the devil "was a murderer from the beginning" (Jn. 8:44). Thus the first murder in history was committed because of Satan's goal to prevent the Redeemer's coming.

The Apostasy of the Human Race

In His war against Satan, God counteracted the murder of Abel by giving Adam and Eve another godly son named Seth (Gen. 4:25). Since this name means "substitute," it is apparent that God meant Seth to be a substitute for Abel.[1] The genealogies found in Genesis 5; 11:10–32; and Luke 3:23–38 reveal that God also intended the Redeemer to come through Seth's line of descent.

It was apparent to Satan that, for every godly son he could destroy, God would raise up another to take his place. Thus Satan changed his tactic. He determined that he would pervert the whole human race, including Seth's line of descent, with apostasy. He began his attack by developing an ungodly line through Cain. Cain and his descendants started to build an advanced civilization that was godless in outlook and was characterized by polygamy and violence (Gen. 4:16–24).

Through time, as Seth's godly line had contact with Cain's ungodly line, it, too, became infected with apostasy. In addition, evil fallen angels ("the sons of God") began to introduce an evil angelic strain into mankind by marrying human women and fathering unique children (Gen. 6:1–4; 2 Pet. 2:4; Jude 6–7). As a result of both these trends, the human race became so perverted that it filled the earth with violence and corruption (Gen. 6:11, 13). As God looked at the situation He "saw that the wickedness of man was great in the earth, and that every imagination of the thoughts of his heart was only evil continually" (Gen. 6:5). God was so grieved that He announced His determination to destroy man from the face of the earth (Gen. 6:6–7).

The Flood

Although Satan had been successful in perverting most of the human race, he was not able to pervert all of it. God counteracted him again by preserving one righteous man who was a descendant of Seth (Gen. 5:6–29; 6:9). The man's name was Noah. In spite of tremendous pressures, Noah stood his ground and refused to be influenced by the apostate attitude and conduct of his contemporaries. God had His man. He was only one man, to be sure, but he was all that was necessary, together with his family, to carry on the godly line of Seth through which the Redeemer was to come.

God was determined to destroy the perverted human race, not just for the purpose of judgment, but also for the purpose of ending the perversion before it could infect even Noah's descendants. Destruction was to be His instrument for preserving the line of the Redeemer so that Satan could not win the war against His kingdom.

God instructed Noah to build a huge ark in which Noah, his family, and representatives of every kind of birds and land animals could escape the coming destruction (Gen. 6:8—7:16). Once the occupants of the ark were safely inside, God caused the entire earth to be inundated by a cataclysmic flood (Gen. 7:10–12). The result was that every human being and every land animal outside the ark were destroyed (Gen. 7:21–23). Thus God counteracted Satan's move to pervert the whole human race so thoroughly that the Redeemer could not come through it.

The New Beginning and the New Apostasy

The flood destroyed the human members of Satan's kingdom. This gave the human race an opportunity for a new beginning with God. After the flood ended, Noah led his family in the worship of God (Gen. 8:20). Because it was the continued existence and influence of a murderer that had begun the perversion of the human race before the flood, God now instituted capital punishment for the purpose of hindering the development of perversion again after the flood (Gen. 9:5–6). This also involved the institution of human government, for a form of government was necessary to inflict the punishment. Thus capital punishment and human government were begun by God as external restraints upon man's tendency toward perversion. Their purpose is to hinder the work of Satan's kingdom in the world. It is for this reason that Paul wrote in Romans 13:1–6,

Let every soul be subject unto the higher powers. For there is no power but of God; the powers that be are ordained of God. Whosoever, therefore, resisteth the power, resisteth the ordinance of God; and they that shall resist shall receive to themselves judgment. For rulers are not a terror to good works, but to the evil. Wilt thou, then, not be afraid of the power? Do that which is good, and thou shalt have praise from the same; for he is the minister of God to thee for good. But if thou do that which is evil, be afraid; for he beareth not the sword in vain; for he is the minister of God, an avenger to execute upon him that doeth evil. Wherefore, ye must needs be in subject, not only for wrath but also for conscience sake. For, for this cause pay ye tribute also; for they are God's ministers attending continually upon this very thing.

In a covenant with Noah, his descendants, and all animals, God promised never again to destroy all flesh with a flood. The rainbow was given as the token of this covenant (Gen. 9:8–17).

Noah uttered a prophecy concerning his descendants (Gen. 9:25–27). This prophecy foretold that God would bestow great blessing upon the line of Noah's son, Shem (Gen. 9:26). Later revelation indicated that the Redeemer would come through Shem's line of descent (Gen. 11:10—12:3).

Satan wanted to make the whole human race, including Shem's redemptive line, apostate again. God had commanded Noah and his descendants to fill the earth with their offspring (Gen. 9:1). Mankind was "not to concentrate in some few spots but" was "to spread out so that the earth" would have "no unoccupied and uncultivated areas."[2] Satan, however, wanted mankind to remain close together in one area, for obvious reasons. First, it is harder to control a mass of people when they are scattered far apart. Second, apostasy spreads faster and easier when people have regular, close contact with one another.

In order to keep people together, one must give them a symbol of unity or a common project to work on. Satan gave Noah's descendants both by prompting them to build a large city and tower on the plain of Babylon to which they had migrated after the flood (Gen. 11:1–4). They were able to contemplate such a project because the entire human race spoke the same language. God counteracted this move toward apostasy by causing the people to speak different languages (Gen. 11:5–7). For the first time in human history more than one language was in existence. As a result of this confusion of language, the building activity halted, and the human race scattered over the earth (Gen. 11:8–9). Those who spoke one language in common separated from those who spoke other languages. They migrated to one part of the earth and began to build a nation on the basis of their common language. For the first time in history different nations began to form (Gen. 10:5, 20, 31–32). Thus the beginning of different languages and nations started as a result of the war between the kingdom of God and the kingdom of Satan. Genesis 11 gives a summary of the geographical distribution of the human race after the confusion of language.[3]

No doubt the scattering of Noah's descendants did slow down the spread of apostasy; however, it did not stop it altogether. Satan was determined to turn all people away from God. Through time Noah's descendants began to suppress the truth about God. They refused to teach succeeding generations about Him, and they rejected the truths concerning God revealed through nature. They boasted that they were wise in doing this, for their denial of God's truth made it appear that man is sovereign. Man's willful apostasy produced two tragic results. First, man invented several idolatrous religions as substitutes for worship of the true God. Second, man degenerated progressively into moral perversion. He gave free reign to vile passions and approved of gross displays of depravity (Rom. 1:18–32). Thus false religions and the most perverted forms of depravity developed as a result of Satan's war against the kingdom of God.

The Abrahamic Covenant

After nations began, God revealed that He intended to bring into existence a new nation, Israel, that would play a key role in

His warfare against the kingdom of Satan. This revelation came in the form of a covenant that God made with a man whose name was changed eventually from Abram to Abraham. Abraham was a member of Shem's line of descent (Gen. 11:10–30). In spite of Satan's new perversion of the human race, God once again had a man who was willing to obey Him (Heb. 11:8).

As a result of God's covenant with him, Abraham moved to Canaan (Gen. 12:1–7). In the covenant, God made three kinds of promises to Abraham: personal, national, and universal. The national promise stated that God would make of Abraham a great nation (Gen. 12:2). The universal promise stated that in Abraham, all the families of the earth would be blessed (Gen. 12:3). This was God's way of promising in veiled terms that the Redeemer, whose redemptive work would bring blessing to all mankind, would come through Abraham's line of descent (Mt. 1:1; Lk. 3:23–24).[4] Thus the Redeemer's line of descent was narrowed down to Abraham and his descendants, the nation of Israel.

The Sojourn in Egypt

After several generations the descendants of Abraham migrated to Egypt (Gen. 46:1–7). As they sojourned there for several centuries, God prospered them greatly (Ex. 1:1–7). By then there could have been no doubt in Satan's mind that Israel was the nation of God's special choosing and that God intended to send the Redeemer and fulfill His purpose for history through Israel. Satan realized that if he wanted to defeat the kingdom of God, he must destroy Israel. In Egypt he began a series of attacks upon Israel that has continued through history to the present day. Thus Satan became the author of anti-Semitism. And anti-Semitism is the result of his war against the kingdom of God.

In his first attempt to annihilate Israel, Satan used the stubborn will of Pharaoh, king of Egypt. Pharaoh devised a fiendish way to destroy Israel systematically (Ex. 1:8–22). Mackintosh wrote of Pharaoh: "Vain man! how little he knows of his real condition and character! He is but the tool of Satan, taken up and used by him, in his malignant efforts to counteract the purposes of God."[5]

God counteracted this satanic move by raising up Moses to lead Israel from Egypt to Canaan and by sending a series of ten plagues upon Egypt to break the will of Pharaoh (Ex. 2:1—12:28).

The Exodus

After the tenth plague, Pharaoh's stubbornness was subdued. He and his people urged the Israelites to leave Egypt (Ex. 12:29–51). Thus the Exodus of Israel from Egypt began. This event proved to be one of the greatest happenings for Israel in Old Testament times.

Israel headed for Canaan. The route that she took led her toward the wilderness of the Sinai Peninsula. This journey afforded Satan several opportunities to attack the nation in various ways. The first attack came shortly after the Exodus began. Pharaoh changed his mind about letting Israel go, so he pursued the nation with his chariot force and army (Ex. 14:1–9). He appeared to have Israel trapped, for the Red Sea blocked her escape (Ex. 14:10–14). God counteracted this threat, however, by dividing the waters of the sea to enable Israel to walk across unhindered. When Pharaoh's chariots gave pursuit, God allowed the divided waters to come together, thereby destroying Egypt's chariot force in short order (Ex. 14:21–31).

The conflict over Israel continued. Satan threatened to destroy the Israelites through lack of water, then tormented them further with water unfit to drink. God counteracted this by revealing to Moses how to make the water fit (Ex. 15:22–26). Next, Satan threatened the nation with starvation, but God provided quail and a daily supply of special food called manna (Ex. 16). Satan attacked with lack of water again, but God supplied water from a rock (Ex. 17:1–7). Satan's next tactic was an attack by the Amalekites, but God gave Israel military victory while Moses prayed (Ex. 17:8–16).

The Mosaic Covenant

Within three months of her departure from Egypt, Israel encamped around Mount Sinai (Ex. 19:1–2). While the nation was there, God established a covenant with her through Moses. This covenant united God and Israel to each other officially (Ex.19:3–8). Although it has been called the Mosaic covenant, it is known more popularly as the Law (Ex. 20:1—23:19).

Because Israel was to be the nation through which the Redeemer would come, it was essential that she be kept free from the apostasy and perverted lifestyle of other nations. In order to insure this freedom, God placed Israel under the Law. The Law was to be an external restraint upon sinful, apostate tendencies until the Redeemer would come (Gal. 3:15—4:5). In order to exercise such restraint, the Law required that those guilty of apostasy and perversion be put to death immediately (Ex. 21:12–17; 22:18–20). The coming of the Redeemer was more crucial for the benefit of mankind than was the life of an individual rebel or pervert.

Whether or not Israel kept the Law, then, was no idle matter. In order to impress this fact upon Israel, God warned the nation that her relationship to the covenant would determine her future course of history. As long as she would keep the covenant, God would bless her more than any other nation and protect her from harm (Lev. 26:3–13; Dt. 28:1–14). On the other hand, if she would break the covenant, God would withdraw His protective presence from her and chasten her with conquest, desolation, and scattering by Gentile nations (Lev. 26:14–39; Dt. 28:15–68). God did promise, however, to preserve a remnant of the nation that would repent of any apostasy (Lev. 26:40–46). Thus the nation never would go out of existence.

The Threat of Apostasy

While Moses was on Mount Sinai communicating with God, Satan attacked the nation again. In the Law God had forbidden the Israelites to make or worship any image of Himself or other gods. Thus Satan knew that any idolatry on Israel's part would stir the wrath of God against her. Therefore, he prompted the Israelites to ask Aaron to make an image that they could worship. Aaron complied, so the people indulged in idolatry and immoral practices (Ex. 32:1–6). God put an end to this apostasy by punishing only those people who had participated in it (Ex. 32:7–35).

The Tabernacle and Sacrifices

Because of Israel's special relationship to God, it was essential that she have a place to worship Him and that He have a place to dwell in a special sense in her midst. To this end God revealed to Moses plans for a portable worship-dwelling structure called the Tabernacle (Ex. 25—31). Once the Tabernacle was built and erected, the glory of God filled it as the sign of God's protective presence in Israel (Ex. 40:34–38). God also gave Israel a system of sacrifices to be offered at the Tabernacle (Lev. 1—7), a priesthood to offer the sacrifices (Lev. 8—10), and a system of worship to be observed (Lev. 11—25). Although the sacrifices could not remove the sins of the people who offered them (Heb. 10:4), they did have teaching value. They taught the Israelites that the only way a sinful person can be brought into right relationship with the holy God is through a substitutionary, blood sacrifice.[6] They also saved them from temporal judgment that would come from breaking certain parts of the Law. Symbolically they pictured ahead of time the coming Redeemer's blood sacrifice of Himself that would take away sin completely and forever (Heb. 10:1, 10—14).

The Failure at Kadesh-Barnea and the Wilderness Wanderings

When Israel arrived at Kadesh-barnea on the border of Canaan, Satan attacked again. He used human fear to produce unbelief, perhaps hoping that this would stir God's wrath to destroy the nation. In spite of God's promises to give them victory over the peoples of Canaan (Ex. 23:20–31), the Israelites panicked when their spies reported that the Canaanites were greater in size than they (Num. 13:25–33). In unbelief they slandered God and decided to return to Egypt (Num. 14:1–10). God countered this unbelief by turning the Israelites back into the Sinai wilderness to wander for forty years until those twenty years old and older would die. The older generations would not enter Canaan (Num. 14:11–35).

During the years of wandering, Israel was attacked again and again by Satan. He used dissatisfaction, boredom, lack of water, and foreign powers as his instruments. As a result, the Israelites rebelled against their leaders (Num. 16) and complained against God (Num. 20:2–13; 21:4–9). Thus Satan tested God's patience, hoping that God would destroy the people through whom the Redeemer was to come. God did judge the nation each time, but He never destroyed her. When these satanic attempts failed, Satan sent Canaanites and then Amorites against Israel to destroy her (Num. 21:1–3, 21–35). God counteracted these attacks by giving Israel military victories. When Israel came to the Plains of Moab, Satan attacked again. Balak, king of Moab, hired the Prophet Balaam to curse Israel so that the Moabites could destroy her. God countered this move by causing the prophet to bless Israel instead of curse her (Num. 22—24).

Satan wasn't finished using the prophet, however. Balaam devised another fiendish way to destroy Israel. He advised Balak to use the Moabite and Midianite women to seduce the Israelites into immorality and idolatry (Num. 31:16). The advice worked. In order to prevent wholesale judgment of Israel, God ordered the guilty Israelite leaders to be hanged immediately.[7] When another Israelite man brought a pagan woman into the nation, a plague broke out among the people. It was stopped when Phinehas the priest killed the man and woman (Num.25:4–8). Thus, through judgment, God ended this new outbreak of apostasy.

When the forty years of wandering were nearly ended, Moses prepared the new generations of Israelites for the conquest of Canaan (Num. 26—36; Dt.). He warned Israel to destroy the peoples living in Canaan (Num. 33:50—34:15). These idolatrous peoples had become so perverted that their cup of iniquity was full and ripe for judgment. They were to be destroyed so that Satan could not use them to drag the Israelites into such gross apostasy and perversion as to make Israel's total destruction necessary (Lev. 18:24–28; Dt. 12:31; 20:17–18). In other words, the coming of the Redeemer was more essential for the benefit of mankind than was the continued existence of the depraved peoples of Canaan.

THE CONFLICT
FROM THE CONQUEST OF CANAAN
THROUGH THE FALL OF JUDAH

The Conquest and Distribution of Canaan

WHEN IT WAS TIME FOR ISRAEL TO cross the Jordan River to invade Canaan, God's work on behalf of the nation became evident again. First, Egypt, which had been controlling Canaan, let go of that control even though she had the resources to continue it.[1] Second, God miraculously stopped the waters of the Jordan River and dried its bed so that Israel could cross over to Canaan (Josh. 3). Third, God appeared in special form to Joshua, Israel's new leader, to give instructions for the conquest of the land and to remind Joshua that victory depended upon God (Josh. 5:13–15).[2]

When God gave Israel its first great victory at Jericho (Josh. 6), Satan attacked. God had commanded the Israelites not to keep anything from Jericho for themselves (Josh. 6:17–19). One man disobeyed. As a result, Israel was defeated soundly when it attacked the next city, Ai. God countered Satan's move to start general disobedience in the nation by ordering the guilty man and his family stoned to death (Josh. 7).

Satan's next attack caught Israel off guard. He was determined to preserve some of the depraved Canaanites so that Israel would be exposed to their degeneracy. The people of the city of Gibeon deceived Israel into believing that they were not Canaanites. Without consulting God first, Israel made a covenant not to destroy the Gibeonites. Thus these pagan people were permitted to remain in the midst of Israel (Josh. 9).

God gave Israel great victories over the southern and northern confederacies of Canaanite city-states (Josh. 10; 11:1–15). Although Israel controlled Canaan, there still were areas and cities within it occupied by Canaanites. It was the responsibility of individual Israelite tribes to clear these out of the portions of land distributed to them.[3]

When the land was distributed, God gave the Levites cities throughout the land. These cities were to be centers of instruction in the Law (Josh. 21:1–42). This was God's way of safeguarding the nation of the Redeemer from apostasy.

Before he died, Joshua warned Israel of the consequences of keeping or breaking the Law, and he exhorted them to keep themselves separate from the pagans and their practices and to serve God (Josh. 23—24). These things were necessary for Israel's survival so that the Redeemer could come.

The Period of the Judges

After Joshua died there was no outstanding, godly man available to lead Israel, and the nation had no centralized government. Satan saw this as an opportune time to press the attack vigorously. As a result, Israel's history was characterized by apostasy and anarchy for the next 350 years.[4] The nation broke God's Law while every man "did that which was right in his own eyes" (Jud. 21:25).

Satan used three kinds of Israelite disobedience to create this tragic situation. First, the people did not rid the land of all the Canaanites as God had commanded (Jud. 1:1—2:5). Second, the Israelites began to adopt the Canaanites' worship of Baal and Ashtaroth (Jud. 2:6—3:4). Third, God's people married Canaanites in direct violation of God's orders (Jud. 3:5–6; Dt. 7:1–5).

As a result of this apostasy, Israelites began to practice gross perversions. Dishonesty, thievery, situation ethics, priests leading idolatrous worship for the sake of money and position, homosexuality, sexual abuse of women to the point of death, and a determination to protect sexual perverts from judgment were the order of the day (Jud. 17—20). During this period of Israel's history, the apostasy never did become nationwide at any one time. Instead, it was sporadic, breaking out in separate areas at different times. No doubt Satan hoped that each beginning of apostasy would spread nationwide, but God stopped it each time before it grew to large proportions. Every time apostasy began, God raised up a foreign power to oppress the apostates until they would repent and return to Him. Upon their repentance God raised up an Israelite deliverer to drive out the oppressor. This cycle of apostasy, oppression, repentance, and deliverance was repeated numerous times throughout the period of the judges (Jud. 3:7—16:31). Thus, although Satan's kingdom did its devilish work repeatedly, God preserved the nation by preventing the apostasy from becoming nationwide.

Samuel's Ministry

In order to end Israel's repeated excursions into apostasy during the period of the judges, God raised up a strong, godly leader for the whole nation. The leader's name was Samuel (1 Sam. 1–3).

Samuel began to minister during days of grave national crisis. The Philistines had defeated Israel and stolen the Ark of the Covenant, and the high priest had died. The nation was in a turmoil. Samuel took control of the situation by calling the nation together and directing the people to repent of their apostasy, put away their false gods, and return to God. All this the people did. As a result, God delivered Israel from all oppressors as long as Samuel lived (1 Sam. 4:1—7:14).

When Samuel became old, he made his sons judges; but they were corrupt. Satan used this corruption to prompt the Israelites to request a king from Samuel. Israel wanted a monarchy with a human king instead of a theocracy with God as King. Samuel protested this sinful decision and warned the people that eventually they would regret having a human king. But the Israelites insisted on having their way (1 Sam. 7:15—8:22). Therefore, God directed Samuel to anoint and present Saul as the first king (1 Sam. 9—10).

Before he retired, Samuel rebuked Israel for her sin and warned her to serve and fear God with all her heart so as not to be consumed (1 Sam. 12). Samuel had been God's "man of the hour" to help preserve the existence of the Redeemer's nation during a very threatening time.

Saul's Apostasy

Satan had a purpose for prompting Israel to ask for a king. While Israel had been without a central government, he had found it impossible to get the whole nation to go apostate at one time. Now that Israel had a king, a central government would be formed. This situation would provide a better opportunity for perverting the entire nation at once. If the king would go apostate, surely the nation would follow suit.

Satan began the attack with the first king. After Saul had been king two years, he began to disobey God and show poor judgment (1 Sam. 13—15). When rebuked for his sins, he excused his actions with a self-justifying spirit. Because of these sins and attitudes, God withdrew His Spirit from Saul and gave it to David, whom God had instructed Samuel to anoint as the new king (1 Sam. 16:1–14).

Saul came under satanic influence (1 Sam. 16:14) and developed three tragic traits: abnormal self-interest, insane jealousy, and full apostasy (1 Sam. 16:14—28:2; 29—30). When the Philistines came to fight Israel, God refused to respond to Saul's appeal for directions. As a result, Saul appealed to a member of Satan's kingdom, a spiritist (1 Sam. 28:3–25). Because of Saul's apostasy, he and his sons died in battle and Israel came under Philistine control (1 Sam. 31). Thus, through death and defeat, God ended this new threat of apostasy.

The Davidic Covenant

After David united the kingdom; captured and made Jerusalem the national, political capital and worship center; and put an end to Philistine domination of Israel (2 Sam. 1—6), he desired to build a permanent house for God in Jerusalem (2 Sam. 7:1–2). It was to be called the Temple.

In response to David's desire, God established a special covenant with him (2 Sam. 7:12–16). In this covenant the Lord made the following promises concerning David:

> First, he was to have a posterity. The covenant explicitly states that he would have a son and that David's house would be established forever. This clearly has reference to David's physical descendants, for David's line would always be the royal line. Secondly, David's throne was to be established forever. Thirdly, David's kingdom was also to be established forever. This has reference to the earthly, political kingdom over Israel.[5]

Later divine revelation and historical events revealed what God meant by "forever." He did not mean that the kingdom of Israel would continue as a political entity in Canaan with a descendant of David as king *without interruption* through the end of history.[6] What He did mean was this: The line of David would continue to exist throughout the rest of history.[7]

Thus, when it would be time for God to establish the theocratic form of His kingdom in the world toward the end of history, a physical descendant of David would be available to set up David's kingdom of Israel in Canaan, to rule that kingdom with David's authority, and to govern the whole world for God.

These promises made the Davidic covenant very significant for the conflict between the kingdom of God and the kingdom of Satan. They meant that Israel never would be annihilated totally at any time in history, and that Israel always would have available to her a legitimate heir to the throne and the potential of becoming an earthly, political kingdom again. Later revelation to the prophets indicated that the Redeemer would be a descendant of David and that the promises of the Davidic covenant would find their ultimate fulfillment in Him. In light of all this, it became imperative to Satan that David's royal line be destroyed.

David's Troubles

God used David to bring Israel to her ancient golden age (2 Sam. 8; 10). With David and Israel enjoying many triumphs, it was time for Satan to strike again. Since the nation and the royal line were his targets, the best place to begin was with the king himself. David committed adultery and murder (2 Sam. 11).

God caused David to be miserable until he finally sobbed out repentance (Ps. 51). Once David repented, God graciously forgave. However, because David and Israel were to play such key roles in the coming of the Redeemer, it was essential that lessons be taught concerning the consequences of such sins. Thus God brought severe troubles to David and the nation (2 Sam. 12—20). This was His way of preventing David's perverted actions from spreading throughout the nation.

Satan attacked again by prompting David to take a military census of the nation (1 Chr. 21). Evidently this numbering was sin because David was motivated by pride and a sense of reliance upon Israel's military strength instead of upon God.[8] God struck at the source of pride and reliance by destroying 70,000 of Israel's men in a pestilence. The pestilence stopped when David repented and offered a sacrifice to God. Thus God ended this satanic sin in the king and nation and reminded them of the source of their strength.

Solomon's Apostasy

Due to the legendary wisdom that God gave him, Solomon brought Israel to her peak of glory and luxury after David died. One of his greatest accomplishments was building the Temple (1 Ki. 5—6). When the Temple was dedicated, the glory of God came to it as a sign of God's special presence there (1 Ki. 8). God covenanted with Solomon to bless Israel greatly as long as she remained faithful to Him, and to drive her out of the land and reject the Temple if the nation were to go apostate (1 Ki. 9:1–9).

Satan still wanted to plunge the whole nation into apostasy and get rid of David's royal line. So once again he began his attack with the king. His philosophy was this: As goes the king, so goes the nation. Solomon built a large chariot and horse force in direct disobedience to God (Dt. 17:15–16). Again, contrary to God's command (Dt. 17:17), he married many wives. Altogether he had 700 wives and 300 concubines (1 Ki. 11:3). Many of these were foreign, idolatrous women whom he married for political expediency. Here again he violated the divine command that Israelites were not to marry foreigners (1 Ki. 11:1–2). These women pressured Solomon to build worship places for their gods in Israel and to worship their idols with them (1 Ki. 11:4–8). Thus the king became apostate. His practice diluted the influence of the Temple and confused the Israelites concerning the difference between God and the false gods.[9]

Because of Solomon's apostasy, God promised to take most of the kingdom away from his son, and He raised up enemies against Solomon in the latter part of his reign (1 Ki. 11:9–40). To one of these enemies, Jeroboam, God promised to give the ten northern tribes to rule (1 Ki. 11:29–39). This was God's way of attempting to isolate the larger part of the nation from the source of apostasy in Judah and to teach the line of David and Judah the folly of apostasy. The coming of the Redeemer was more important than the unity of the nation. In order to prevent God from doing this, Satan used Solomon to try to kill Jeroboam, but Jeroboam escaped (1 Ki. 11:40).

The Division of the Kingdom

Through the folly of Solomon's son, Rehoboam, the ten northern tribes revolted and set up their own government with Jeroboam as king (1 Ki. 12:1–24). Thus the united kingdom divided into two kingdoms: the kingdom of Israel in the north and the kingdom of Judah in the south.

The Decline and Fall of the Northern Kingdom

Satan was not content to have apostasy exist just in the southern kingdom. He used fear as his instrument for introducing apostasy to the northern kingdom. Jeroboam feared that, if his people were to continue to worship at the Temple in Judah, eventually they would give back their allegiance to Rehoboam. To prevent this Jeroboam erected two idols and established a counterfeit priesthood and false religious system for the northern kingdom. He himself led the northern Israelites in this apostate worship (1 Ki. 12:25–33). Because Jeroboam persisted in this apostasy, God promised to smite the northern kingdom and to send it into captivity beyond the Euphrates River (1 Ki. 13:1—14:16).

Although the northern kingdom adopted apostasy later than Judah, it pursued its most gross forms more persistently than Judah. The northern kingdom had a total of nineteen kings during its history. Every one of these kings was apostate in character and action. The worst king was Ahab, whose wife was the devilish Phoenician princess named Jezebel (1 Ki. 21:25–26; 16:31). Under Jezebel's influence, Ahab built a temple to Baal in the capital city, made Baal worship the official religion of the kingdom, imported and supported 850 prophets of Baal and Astarte, murdered most of God's prophets, and abolished the worship of God.

God countered the apostasy by sending several prophets and different forms of judgment to the northern kingdom as warnings to repent. The prophets declared that, if Israel would not repent, God would raise up a foreign power to smite her and to carry her into captivity (Hos. 11:5; Amos 6:14; 9:8–10).

In spite of the many warnings and judgments, the people of Israel refused to repent. So God raised up Assyria to be His instrument for chastening His apostate people (Isa. 10:5–6). Assyria invaded the northern kingdom in 734 and 732 B.C., took control of Galilee and the land east of Jordan, carried into captivity Israelites from those regions, and made a vassal of the Israelite king (2 Ki. 15:29).[10] After the northern kingdom rebelled and made an alliance with Egypt, the Assyrians came again in 725 B.C. and besieged the capital city, Samaria, until it surrendered in 722 B.C. The Israelites were carried captive to the regions of Persia.[11] This ended the northern kingdom. Because of its persistent apostasy, it lasted little more than two centuries (931–722 B.C.).[12]

The Decline and Fall of the Southern Kingdom

Rehoboam and most of his successors followed the poor example of Solomon and plunged the kingdom of Judah deeper into apostasy. Throughout its history the southern kingdom had a total of nineteen kings and one queen. Of these twenty rulers, only seven were godly.

While Satan was working to prevent the Redeemer from coming by pushing Judah deeper into apostasy, he also worked to accomplish the same goal by trying to annihilate the royal line of David. His instrument of attack was Athaliah, daughter of Ahab and Jezebel, the notorious duo of the northern kingdom. Athaliah married into the royal house of Judah (2 Ki. 8:16–18). After her husband and son died, she seized the throne of Judah and made herself queen. To secure her position as ruler, she ordered the extermination of every royal person descended from David (2 Ki. 11:1).[13]

God countered this satanic attempt to destroy the line of the Redeemer by preserving one of David's royal descendants. The infant Joash was hidden in the Temple for six years by the high priest and his wife (2 Chr. 22:11–12). At the right time Joash was crowned king, and Athaliah was slain (2 Ki. 11:4–16).

God counteracted the growth of apostasy in Judah by prompting several revivals through godly kings. The greatest revival took place under Hezekiah. Because of this return to God, the Lord kept His promise, delivered by Moses centuries earlier, to protect His people from harm. In 701 B.C. a huge Assyrian army invaded Judah.[14] When it threatened to besiege Jerusalem, God killed 185,000 Assyrian soldiers in one night, thereby forcing the remainder of the army to return home (2 Ki. 18:9—19:37).

Because of the occasional revivals, Judah lasted longer than the northern kingdom. However, in spite of these revivals, the most persistent trend of Judah was into apostasy. Once again God raised up prophets and various forms of judgment to warn His people to repent, but once again the people refused to heed them. Apostasy reached its lowest depth during the long reign of Manasseh, Judah's most wicked king (2 Ki. 21:1–18). Manasseh led his kingdom into more perverted practices than those of the Canaanites. The apostasy of his reign became so gross that God's judgment of Judah was made irrevocable. Even a later revival under Josiah could not cancel it out (2 Ki. 23:26–27; 24:3–4).

After Assyria fulfilled God's purpose for her—the chastening of the northern kingdom of Israel—she continually declined in power. Because God no longer needed her for His service, she was crushed completely by the Medes and Babylonians by 605 B.C.[15] With Judah's cup of apostasy rising to the full mark, it was time for God to raise up a new foreign power to be His instrument of chastening. That new power was Babylon.

After he crushed Assyria, Nebuchadnezzar, the crown prince of Babylon, led his armies into Judah in 605 B.C. and claimed treasures and hostages in Jerusalem. The Prophet Daniel and his friends were among the hostages carried captive to Babylon (2 Ki. 24:1; Dan. 1:1–6).[16] Thus the Babylonian Captivity of the Jewish people began.

In 597 B.C. the Babylonian armies returned to Jerusalem, stripped the Temple, and took the royal treasures of Judah. The king of Judah, other political and cultural leaders, and Ezekiel the prophet were carried captive in this second deportation of Jewish people to Babylon (2 Ki. 24:8–16).[17]

After Ezekiel arrived in Babylon, God somehow caused him to witness the withdrawal of His glory from the Temple and city of Jerusalem (Ezek. 8—11). This was a very significant event in the war between the kingdom of God and kingdom of Satan. It signified the withdrawal of God's protective presence from the midst of His people because of their persistent apostasy. Now the way was open for the Babylonians to destroy the Temple and Jerusalem.

Due to the rebellion of their puppet Judean king, the Babylonians returned to Jerusalem. In 586 B.C. they entered the city, slaughtered many Jews, destroyed the Temple, left the city in ruins, and carried most of the remaining Jewish people captive to Babylon (2 Ki. 25:1–11).[18] Thus the kingdom of Judah came to an end after an existence of nearly 350 years (931–586 B.C.).[19]

One thing should be noted about the fall of Israel and Judah. Because of His holiness, God did permit many of His people to be slaughtered for their apostasy. However, He did not permit the nation to be annihilated totally. He preserved a remnant. The punishment of His people was intended to cure them of their apostasy so that the Redeemer could come.

THE CONFLICT
FROM THE BABYLONIAN CAPTIVITY
THROUGH THE ASCENSION OF CHRIST

The Babylonian Captivity

ONCE THE JEWISH PEOPLE WERE captive in Babylon, Satan attacked again. Nebuchadnezzar decreed that all his subjects should worship an image of himself (Dan. 3:1–7). Jewish obedience to this decree would have involved God's people in apostasy again. God countered this satanic move by miraculously preserving through their punishment the first Israelites who refused to obey the king's decree (Dan. 3:8–27). As a result, the Jewish people were released from any obligation to worship anyone except God (Dan. 3:28–30).

After Babylon fulfilled God's purpose for her—the chastening of Judah—God no longer needed her for His service. As the end of the Babylonian Captivity drew near, Babylon fell suddenly to Medo-Persia in 539 B.C. (Dan. 5).[1] In fulfillment of Isaiah 44:28 and 45:1, Cyrus, king of Persia, issued a decree in 538 or 537 B.C. permitting the Israelites to return to their homeland to rebuild the Temple.[2] This decree ended the Babylonian Captivity.

The Persian Period

The majority of Jewish people decided to remain in Babylon after the captivity ended. However, nearly 50,000 did return to their homeland under the leadership of Zerubbabel and Jeshua (Ezra 1—2). Upon their arrival in the homeland, the returning Jews built an altar and reinstituted the feasts and offerings prescribed in the Law (Ezra 3:1–7). In the second year of their return they began to rebuild the Temple (Ezra 3:8–13). At this juncture, Satan attacked again.

Inasmuch as it would be easier to lead the Israelites into apostasy if they didn't have a permanent place to worship God, Satan desired to prevent the rebuilding of the Temple. Samaritan enemies of the Jews resisted the rebuilding of the Temple so severely that all building activity ceased for at least sixteen years (Ezra 4:1–5, 24). God counteracted this satanic move by raising up two prophets, Haggai and Zechariah, to exhort the people to continue rebuilding the Temple. As a result, the building activity began again in 520 B.C. (Ezra 5:1–2).[3]

Satan threatened to stop the building again through a letter sent to King Darius of Persia by more enemies of the Jewish people (Ezra 5:3–17). God countered this move through the king. Darius found Cyrus' decree concerning the Temple, then ordered the Jews' enemies not to interfere with the building activity but to give the Jewish people material assistance for the Temple. Darius even threatened to execute anyone who hindered the project (Ezra 6:1–12). Thus the Jewish people finished the Temple in 516 B.C. (Ezra 6:13–16).

During the reign of King Xerxes (486–465 B.C.), Satan attempted again to annihilate the people through whom the Redeemer was to come.[4] Haman, the prime minister of Persia, persuaded the king to decree that all Jews should be executed on a certain day (Esther 3:7–15). God countered this attack by bringing the king to authorize a new decree permitting the Jewish people to defend themselves at the prescribed time of execution (Esther 4—9). Thus God's people were preserved.

Satan was determined to get the Jews in the Promised Land involved in apostasy again. Inasmuch as Israel had gone apostate on a grand scale several centuries earlier through the marriage of Israelite men to foreign, pagan, women, there was good reason to believe that the same method could work again. In violation of the

Law numerous Jewish men, including Temple priests and political leaders, married foreign, pagan women. These forbidden unions led the nation into idolatrous practices once more (Ezra 9:1–2). God countered this new outbreak of apostasy by sending Ezra, a teacher of the Law, to the land in 458 B.C. with a decree from King Artaxerxes I. This decree commanded Ezra to establish a centralized government in Jerusalem, teach God's Law to the Israelites in the land, and punish any Jewish people who refused to obey it (Ezra 7). Ezra ordered the Jewish men to repent of their sin and to put away their pagan wives (Ezra 10). Thus the spread of apostasy was stopped.

In 445 B.C. Nehemiah received from Artaxerxes I a decree granting permission and aid to rebuild the walls of Jerusalem.[5] As long as the walls remained broken down, the Jews in the land remained subject to great affliction and reproach; therefore, it was to Satan's advantage to keep the walls down. Thus the Israelites' enemies tried to prevent the rebuilding of the walls through derision and threat of armed aggression. But God used Nehemiah to urge the Jews to build with weapons in hand. Next, the enemies laid traps to get rid of Nehemiah, but God gave him wisdom to avoid them. Thus the walls were rebuilt in fifty-two days (Neh. 1—7).

Satan continued to persist. After a while, pagan people were allowed to live with the Jews in the land. A former pagan enemy was given a Temple chamber in which to live; the Israelites stopped paying the tithe, thereby causing the Temple to be deserted by its ministers; merchants were allowed to desecrate the Sabbath by conducting business on that day in Jerusalem; Jewish men married pagan women again; the people offered blemished sacrifices to God; the priests dishonored God by their actions; the Jewish men divorced their wives; and the people called evil good and concluded that it was useless to serve God (Neh. 13; Mal.). God countered all these evil tendencies through the preaching of the Prophet Malachi and the reforms instituted by Nehemiah.

The Message of the Prophets

The Old Testament prophets foretold many things concerning the coming Redeemer. They pictured Him in two major ways: as the suffering Servant who would die to pay the penalty of man's sin (Isa. 52:13—53:12), and as the glorious King who would establish the theocratic rule of God's kingdom over the world again (Isa. 9:6–7; Dan. 7:13–14).

The prophets revealed that, when the Redeemer would establish the future theocratic kingdom, He would begin to reverse all the tragic consequences of man's sin. For example, He would change animal nature, so all animals would be completely tame again (Isa. 11:6–9; 65:25); He would reverse the effects of death by healing all diseases and deformities (Isa. 33:24; 35:5–6), eliminating hazards (Ezek. 34:25–29), and increasing man's lifespan (Isa. 65:20, 22). He would restore the fertility of the earth to such an extent that there would be a great growth and fruitage of trees (Isa. 55:13; Ezek. 47:12; Joel 2:21–22), a huge multitude of fish (Ezek. 47:9–10), an abundance of grain and wine (Joel 2:24; Amos 9:13), and such a superabundant supply of food in general that famine would be abolished (Jer. 31:12–14; Ezek. 34:27–29; 36:29–30; 47:12; Joel 2:24–26; Zech. 8:11–12). He would control the environment for the benefit of man (Ezek. 34:26–27), even healing its pollution (Ezek. 47:1–12); and He would abolish war and injustice (Isa. 2:2–4; 9:6–7; 11:2–5; Jer. 23:5; Mic. 4:1–3; Zech. 9:9–10).

The prophets called the coming Redeemer the Anointed One (Ps. 2) or Messiah (Dan. 9:25–26) and indicated that He would rule God's future, theocratic kingdom as a descendant of David, sitting on David's throne (Isa. 9:6–7; Jer. 23:5–6; 30:9; 33:14–17; Ezek. 34:23–24; 37:24–25). Thus He would fulfill the Davidic covenant (Jer. 33:20–26).

Finally, the prophets declared that the coming theocratic kingdom would not be set up until Israel would repent or turn back to God (Dt. 30:1–10; Jer. 31:16–40; Ezek. 36:32–38; Hos. 3:4–5; Zech. 13:9). Thus, the nation of Israel is a key to the establishment of the earthly, political form of the kingdom of God.

The Grecian Period

Persia served God's purpose for her—the restoration and reestablishment of the Jewish people to their homeland. Once that purpose was fulfilled, God no longer needed her for His service. Thus in 334 B.C. the Persian Empire was invaded by a Greco-Macedonian army under the leadership of Alexander the Great.[6] By 331 B.C. the Persian Empire had been totally consumed by the new empire from Greece.[7]

Alexander pushed his armies as far east as the Punjab area of India.[8] When his soldiers could not keep up the intense forced marches, Alexander discharged them in groups. Many of these men "settled where they were discharged, married native women, and raised their families."[9] As a result, a common language and culture were established "from east to west and down into Egypt," and they were the Greek language and culture.[10]

After Alexander died suddenly in 323 B.C., his empire experienced internal struggles as his generals and their successors fought for control.[11] Eventually Ptolemy and his successors gained control of Egypt and Israel, while Syria, Babylonia, and Asia Minor went to the House of Seleucus.[12]

The Jewish people fared well under the Ptolemies. But after the Seleucids of Syria captured the Holy Land from the Ptolemies in 199 B.C., their situation changed drastically.[13] Satan attacked the people of the Redeemer again. One of the Seleucid rulers, Antiochus Epiphanes (175–163 B.C.), was determined to impose a common Greek culture and religion upon his whole kingdom.[14] This involved an attempt to stamp out the Jewish worship of God. To accomplish his goal, Antiochus abolished Jewish sacrifices.[15] He entered the holy of holies of the Temple and desecrated it, sacrificed a sow on the altar of burnt offering, and outlawed circumcision and Sabbath observance.[16] He erected heathen altars, enforced pagan sacrifices, instituted the worship of Zeus and other Greek deities, and executed any Jews found with a copy of the Law.[17] Compliance with these policies involved God's people in apostasy again.

One party of Jewish people accepted the policies of Antiochus enthusiastically. This party received its leadership from the priestly aristocracy.[18] Eventually this group became known as Sadducees.[19] God counteracted this move toward apostasy through the Orthodox party of Jews. Under the leadership of a family of men called the Maccabees, this party fought Antiochus and his forces until religious freedom was won and the Temple worship fully restored in 164 B.C.[20] Eventually the Orthodox group became known as Pharisees.[21]

The Beginning of the Roman Period

Greece fulfilled God's purpose for her—the provision of a universal language for the Mediterranean Sea world. Later this common language would facilitate the spread of the gospel and the New Testament Scriptures. After the Greek Empire completed her service, she fell to Rome. In 63 B.C. the Holy Land came under Roman domination.[22] Eventually the Romans appointed Herod the Great to be king of Judea for them. Herod began his reign in 37 B.C.[23]

The Life and Ministry of Jesus Christ

Although Satan tried repeatedly either to destroy Israel or to make her totally apostate throughout Old Testament times, God continually preserved a faithful remnant of His people. Finally, through a young woman who was a member of that remnant, the Redeemer came. An angel announced to Mary that her Son was to be called Jesus, the Son of the most High, and that He would receive the throne of His father David and a kingdom that would last forever (Lk. 1:26–33).

Jesus Christ was born around 5 or 4 B.C.[24] Thus, "when the fulness of time came, God sent forth" the Redeemer, "born of a woman," just as He had promised in Genesis 3:15 (Gal. 4:4). Despite his many frantic attempts to prevent the Redeemer from coming, Satan had failed. The Person who was the key to the fulfillment of God's purpose for history was now present on earth. He had become human flesh for the purpose of putting away man's sin by the substitutionary sacrifice of Himself so that He could crush Satan and the works of his kingdom (Jn. 1:1, 14, 29; Heb. 2:14; 9:26; 1 Jn. 3:8).

Now that the Redeemer had come, Satan's goal was to prevent the Redeemer from dying the substitutionary death and from establishing God's theocratic kingdom. Satan tried several methods to accomplish his goal. For one thing, he tried more than once to destroy the Redeemer before He could finish His work. Not long after Jesus was born in Bethlehem, King Herod, in an attempt to kill the new Davidic King, ordered the slaughter of infants in that city (Mt. 2:16). God countered that move by forewarning the Redeemer's stepfather to flee with Him to Egypt (Mt. 2:13–15). When Jesus preached to His hometown people for the first time, they became so enraged that they tried to kill Him (Lk. 4:16–29). Jesus countered that attempt by miraculously walking through their midst unharmed (Lk. 4:30). On at least two other occasions some Jews attempted to stone Jesus to death, but He escaped (Jn. 8:59; 10:31, 39). The Redeemer recognized that these attempts on His life were prompted by Satan's kingdom (Jn. 8:37–47).

A second method of attack that Satan used against the Redeemer was apostasy. If he could get Jesus to depart from God's purpose for Him, he could accomplish his goal. Apostasy had worked well with the human race and Israel; he hoped it would work with the Redeemer. To this end, Satan tempted Jesus in the wilderness (Mt. 4:1–11). In one of the temptations Satan offered to give Jesus all the kingdoms of the world if He would bow down and worship him (Mt. 4:8–9). This was Satan's way of offering Jesus the rule of the world system without the sufferings of the cross. Had Jesus accepted the offer, Satan would have disrupted God's purpose for history. In response to Satan's offer, Jesus rebuked him and refused to become apostate (Mt. 4:10).

Satan tried more than once to make the Redeemer abort His mission (Lk. 4:13). Once he used Peter to try to persuade Jesus to avoid the cross, but again Jesus rebuked him (Mt. 16:21–23). In spite of all his efforts, Satan could not make the Redeemer become apostate. As a result, on the night before His crucifixion, Jesus could say that the prince of the world had nothing in Him (Jn. 14:30). Jesus had rejected every scheme that would make Him a party to Satan's cause. Thus it was only a matter of time until Satan would be cast out of his sphere of authority in the world (Jn. 12:31). During His earthly ministry, Jesus offered the promised theocratic kingdom to Israel. As noted earlier, the prophets declared that the theocratic kingdom would not be set up until Israel would meet the spiritual requirement of repentance. For this reason John the Baptist, who prepared the way for the coming of the Redeemer, Jesus, and the disciples all preached the same message: "Repent ye; for the kingdom of heaven is at hand" (Mt. 3:1–2; 4:17; Mk. 6:7–13). Since Israel was a key to the establishment of the kingdom, Jesus commanded His disciples not to go to the Gentiles or Samaritans, but only to Israel (Mt. 10:5–7). For the same reason, when Jesus was approached by a Gentile woman for help, He said, "I was not sent but unto the lost sheep of the house of Israel" (Mt. 15:21–26).

Through His miracles Jesus demonstrated that right then Israel had in her midst the One who possessed the powers necessary to establish the kingdom. When He cast out demons, He demonstrated His ability to devastate the kingdom of Satan (Mt. 12:22–30). His miracles of casting demons into pigs and causing a fish with a shekel in its mouth to come to Peter displayed His ability to control animal nature (Mt. 17:24–27; Mk. 5:1–20). His healing of all kinds of diseases and deformities (Mk. 3:1–6; 7:31–37; Jn. 5:1–9; 9:1–41) and raising of dead people to life (Mt. 9:18–26; Lk. 7:11–17; Jn. 11:1–44) revealed His ability to reverse the effects of death. When He cursed a fig tree and caused it to die (Mt. 21:18–22), produced huge multitudes of fish (Lk. 5:1–11; Jn. 21:19), turned water into wine (Jn. 2:1–11), and expanded small amounts of food to feed crowds of 5,000 and 4,000 (Mk. 8:1–9; Jn. 6:5–14), He demonstrated His ability to produce the great fruitage of trees, multitude of fish, abundance of wine, and superabundance of food that the prophets declared would characterize the theocratic kingdom. His calming of storms and walking on water displayed His power to eliminate hazards and control the environment for the benefit of man (Mt. 14:24–33; Mk. 4:35–41).

It is interesting to note that, when Jesus sent out His disciples to preach repentance and the kingdom to Israel, He gave them power to perform miracles characteristic of conditions to come in the literal, earthly, theocratic kingdom (Mk. 6:7–13; Mt. 10:5–8). The purpose of Jesus' and the disciples' miracles was twofold: first, to point out Jesus as the One who could establish the theocratic kingdom with its regeneration of the earth (Mt. 19:28) and, second, to substantiate the declaration that the kingdom could be set up if Israel would repent as a nation. Thus the Jewish people who saw these miracles were receiving a foretaste of the miraculous powers that will be characteristic of the future Millennial age (Heb. 6:5).

Satan hated the preaching of the kingdom message. He knew that if Israel were to believe the declaration and repent, he and his kingdom would be crushed. Therefore, it was imperative to him that the nation reject the offer of the kingdom. To this end he worked diligently in the hearts of Jewish people to prevent the message from taking root and bearing fruit in them (Mt. 13:18–22). The end result was that the majority of Jews did not believe the declaration concerning the kingdom. They wanted the literal, political, theocratic kingdom (Mk. 11:8–10), but they didn't want to meet the spiritual requirement necessary to have it. They felt that, because they were Abraham's descendants, they didn't need to repent (Mt. 3:7–9). Thus the nation of Israel rejected the offer of the theocratic kingdom.

By prompting Israel to reject the offer of the kingdom, Satan ironically sealed his own doom (Jn. 12:31; 16:11). In accordance with His sovereign plan for the world, God used Israel's rejection as His means of providing the substitutionary sacrifice for man's sin (Jn. 12:37–40; Acts 2:22–23; 4:27–28). Israel rejected the offer of the kingdom by rejecting the Redeemer who made the offer (Jn. 12:37–38). In its rejection of Jesus as its King, Israel cried for His crucifixion (Jn. 19:13–16). When Jesus was crucified, He died as "the Lamb of God, [that] taketh away the sin of the world" (Jn. 1:29). His death paid the price that satisfied or propitiated divine justice (Rom. 3:24–25; 1 Jn. 2:2; 4:10).

In light of this, Jesus' statement, "It is finished," at the end of His cross experience, was most significant. John stated that He made this statement after knowing that all things were finished (Jn. 19:28–30). This statement meant that, through His crucifixion, the Redeemer had finished the work that was necessary for God to fulfill His purpose for history—the crushing of Satan and his kingdom, the establishment of the theocratic kingdom, and the reversal of the tragic consequences of man's sin. This statement must have sent a shudder through Satan. In spite of all his efforts to prevent the Redeemer from coming and doing His work, he had failed. The sovereignty of God had overruled.

On the third day after His crucifixion, Jesus rose bodily from the dead (Mt. 28:1–10; 1 Cor. 15:3–4). His resurrection was significant for several reasons. First, it was evidence that His death, as a substitutionary sacrifice for man's sin, had satisfied the divine justice of God. Had God not been satisfied, He would not have raised Jesus (Acts 2:24). Second, it proved that the Redeemer had won for man a victory over death and over Satan, who has the power of death (1 Cor. 15:20–24; Heb. 2:14). Third, it was the assurance that the establishment of the theocratic kingdom had not been abandoned by God. When Jesus died, His disciples lost hope that He would establish the theocratic kingdom (Lk. 24:13–21). The resurrection made the Redeemer available again to set up and rule the kingdom at God's appointed time (Acts 1:3, 6–7).

For forty days Jesus gave proof of His bodily resurrection by making numerous appearances (Lk. 24:36–43; Acts 1:3; 1 Cor. 15:3–7). At the end of those days He ascended into heaven (Mk. 16:19; Lk. 24:51; Acts 1:9–11), there to remain until Israel would repent (Mt. 23:37–39).

5

THE CONFLICT
FROM THE REMOVAL OF ISRAEL
FROM THE PLACE OF BLESSING
THROUGH THE REFORMATION

The Removal of Israel
From the Place of Blessing

WHEN ISRAEL REJECTED HER MESSIAH, the promised Redeemer, it was obvious that she was not prepared to make herself right with God through repentance. The Scriptures make it clear, however, that eventually the day will come when the nation will repent. At that time the Redeemer will return and set up the theocratic kingdom, bringing to the earth "seasons of refreshing" and "the times of restoration of all things" that God promised through the prophets (Acts 3:19–21; cf. Ezek. 36:25–38; Zech. 12:10—13:2).

Because of Israel's attitude of unbelief toward Jesus, God removed her temporarily from the place of blessing that He had given her centuries before through the Mosaic Covenant. Israel will continue to remain outside that place of blessing until she repents by believing in Jesus Christ. Until that time comes, God is doing a special work among the Gentiles, bringing many of them to salvation from sin (Rom. 11:11–27).

The Anti-Semitism of the Present Dispensation

Because Israel rejected her Messiah, she doomed herself to centuries of desolation and persecution at the hands of the

Gentiles (Mt. 23:37–38; Lk. 19:41–44). This persecution will continue until the nation is willing to change its mind about Jesus Christ (Mt. 23:39). Being outside the place of blessing, Israel cannot rely upon God to protect her from all harm. Her unbelief has exposed her to vicious anti-Semitism.

It would appear that Satan is the one who prompts the anti-Semitism even of this present dispensation. Although Israel is in a state of spiritual rebellion against God, she still is a key to the establishment of the theocratic kingdom. Being aware of the fact that he will not be crushed and the kingdom will not be set up until Israel repents, Satan has been striving to prevent that repentance. The surest way to prevent it is to annihilate Israel before she can repent. Thus, throughout this present dispensation, one of Satan's goals has been the destruction of Israel.

In trying to accomplish his goal Satan has used several agencies for anti-Semitism. In ancient times he used the Roman Empire to slaughter thousands of Jews while Rome crushed their rebellions. During the Middle Ages he used the predominant, organized church to institute the Inquisition against the Jewish people. In the era of the Second World War he used Nazi Germany to annihilate some six million Jews in Europe. Later he used Communism in Russia. Ultimately it is Satan's desire to destroy Israel that lies behind the Arab-Israeli conflict in the Middle East.

Although God permits Israel to be chastened in this manner for her unbelief, He does not permit the total annihilation of the nation. The Jewish people are a vital key to the fulfillment of His purpose for history; therefore, God is careful to preserve at least a remnant throughout history, just as He had promised (Jer. 30:9–11; 46:27–28; Ezek. 6:8; 14:21–23; 36:16–31; Rom. 9:27–28).

The Birth of the Church

God never allows the world to go on without a witness concerning Himself and His universal kingdom. With Israel being out of joint spiritually, God was determined to raise up a new witnessing agency. Instead of being comprised of one nation, this new agency was to consist of people from many nations and tongues. Instead of being limited just to Jewish people, its membership was to include believing Jews and Gentiles, bound together in harmony as one body (Eph. 2:11—3:11). This new agency was to be known as the Church, the body and bride of Christ (Mt. 16:18; 1 Cor. 12:12–27; Eph. 4:4–6; 5:22–32). It was to continue in the world until God would begin to work with Israel again to bring her to repentance.

Immediately before His ascension, Jesus delivered a special commission for the Church: "Go ye into all the world, and preach the gospel to the whole creation" (Mk. 16:15). He also promised to give the Church the power to perform this witnessing ministry by giving it the Holy Spirit (Lk. 24:49; Acts 1:8). Several days after Jesus' ascension, the Holy Spirit came on the day of Pentecost, and the Church was born (Acts 2; 11:15).

Early Attacks Against the Church

With the birth of the Church, Satan had a new enemy to contend with. The Church's preaching of the gospel posed a serious threat to his kingdom. Every time the gospel is preached to members of Satan's kingdom, they are in danger of believing it. Such belief transfers a person out of Satan's kingdom of darkness and into the universal kingdom of God (Acts 26:17–18; Gal. 1:4; Col. 1:13). Thus, in order to prevent the membership of his kingdom from being depleted, Satan determined to blind the minds of his people to the gospel (2 Cor. 4:3–4) and attack the Church.

Satan's attacks have had two major thrusts. On the one hand, he assaults individual members of the Church by tempting them (Acts 5:3; 1 Th. 3:5), accusing them (Rev. 12:10), persecuting them to the point of death (Rev. 2:10; 1 Pet. 5:8), hindering their work (1 Th. 2:18), trying to defeat them (Eph. 6:10–20), and deceiving them into believing wrong things by sowing among them his people who fashion themselves as ministers of righteousness (Mt. 13:38–39; 2 Cor. 11:13–15). It is because of Satan's war against Christians that they are exhorted to endure hardness as good soldiers of Jesus Christ (2 Tim. 2:3–4), to put on the whole armor of God (Eph. 6:10–18), and to resist Satan (Jas. 4:7; 1 Pet. 5:8–9). Thus God counters Satan's attacks by giving Christians adequate equipment and instruction.

On the other hand, Satan attacks the Church as an organized institution. Very shortly after the Church had begun, Satan tried to annihilate it through persecution. In spite of the fact that the church was totally Jewish in membership in its beginning years, it was attacked by Jewish enemies of the gospel. The apostles were imprisoned (Acts 4—5; 12); Stephen was stoned to death (Acts 6:8—7:60); James, the brother of John, was slain with a sword (Acts 12:2); and James, the half-brother of Jesus, had his brains dashed out with a club.[1]

The early phase of Jewish persecution was organized and executed by a young Jew named Saul. Saul wreaked havoc on the Church (Acts 8:1–3; 9:1–2). God countered this satanic persecution by converting Saul to Christianity while he was on the road to Damascus to persecute more Christians (Acts 9:1–22). Eventually Saul became Paul, the great apostle to the Gentiles (Acts 13:9; 9:15). Thus the greatest opponent of the gospel became the foremost proponent of it. Sometime after Saul's conversion, Herod Agrippa took over the leadership of the persecution of the Church, but God countered that by causing Herod to die a premature death (Acts 12:1, 21–23).

While Satan attacked the Church outwardly with persecution, he assaulted it inwardly with apostate teachings. False teachers penetrated the Church with such heresies as legalism, gnosticism, and antinomianism (Acts 20:29–30). God counteracted this move toward apostasy through the apostles, who taught and wrote against these false views (Gal.; Col.; 1 and 2 Jn.; Jude), and through the decision of the apostles and elders at the Council of Jerusalem (Acts 15).

The Roman Persecution

The Jewish persecutors were not able to destroy the Church. In fact, the more they persecuted the Church, the more the

Church grew (Acts 8:1, 4–8, 25, 40; 11:19–21; 12:24; 13:49). Thus, in order to accomplish his goals of annihilation and apostasy, Satan turned to the greatest military power on earth—Rome.

Nero (54–68 A.D.) was the first Roman emperor to persecute the Church.[2] He turned Christians into living torches to illuminate his gardens at night.[3] He also was responsible for having Paul beheaded and perhaps Peter crucified head downward.[4]

Prior to 250 A.D. most of the Roman persecutions were local and sporadic.[5] From 250 A.D. on they became universal in scope.[6] Christians were ordered to participate in worship of the emperor and pagan gods.[7] Such worship involved apostasy for God's people. When many Christians refused to comply, the government made the total annihilation of the Church and its Scriptures an empire goal.[8] Satan was determined to destroy not only God's people but also God's book that foretold his defeat. The cruel persecution and execution of Christians were carried out systematically. Thousands were martyred for their faith.

God countered the persecutions by using them to His own advantage. Once again, the more the Church was persecuted, the more it grew. In fact, the Church grew so amazingly during the persecutions that Tertullian, a church leader who lived during the time, made a statement saying that the blood of the martyrs was the seed of the Church.[9]

The Church's Apostasy

In 311 A.D. Emperor Galerius issued an edict granting toleration to the Church.[10] Then Emperor Constantine granted total freedom to Christianity through the Edict of Milan in 313 A.D.[11] By 324 A.D. Christianity had become the officially favored religion of the empire.[12] Finally, in 380 A.D., Emperor Theodosius I issued an edict that made Christianity the official and only religion allowed within the empire.[13] Now the government began persecuting other religions.

At first the transition from being the persecuted to being the exclusive religion of the state appeared to be a tremendous victory for the Church. However, time was to prove that the "victory" was a defeat in disguise. Satan recognized the union of church and state as a golden opportunity to introduce apostasy to the Church. Once Christianity was made the only religion allowed, local churches became swamped with large masses of pagans who wanted to become "Christians." Through this contact the pagans found the worship of the churches to be considerably different from that of their temples. Whereas the pagans had bowed and prayed to images of their gods, goddesses, and national heroes, the churches had no images. The pagans had had one goddess whom they adored as the queen of heaven; they also had had numerous heathen festivals, blood sacrifices, and priests. The churches had none of these. Because of these differences, the church seemed irrelevant to the pagans.

Christians feared that, unless the church were made relevant to the pagans, they never would be reached for Christ. In order to make the church relevant, these Christians attempted to Christianize the pagan practices and then adopted them into the church. They substituted images of the apostles and martyrs for images of gods, goddesses, and national heroes. Veneration of Mary as the queen of heaven replaced veneration of the pagan queen. Communion was changed from a memorial to a sacrifice; elders were transformed from teachers into priests, and heathen festivals were incorporated as special church days.[14]

At first it appeared that this process of adopting the methods of Satan's kingdom in order to reach the members of that kingdom was correct. Local churches swelled numerically as the pagans professed to be Christians now that the churches seemed more relevant to them. However, time was to demonstrate that most of these people were still pagans at heart—Christianized pagans to be sure, but still pagans. The end result was that the churches became largely pagan in practice and membership. Through time, "ambitious, worldly, unscrupulous men sought office in the church for social and political influence."[15] In western Europe they built the church into a monstrous religious-political machine that gradually usurped power over the state.[16] Thus the organized church of the Middle Ages became characterized, not by true, biblical *Christianity*, but by "a more or less corrupt *hierarchy* controlling the nations of Europe."[17]

As organized Christendom became more apostate, even the true gospel became perverted. The Scriptures had revealed and the apostles had taught that salvation was solely by God's grace through personal faith in the Person and work of Jesus Christ (Rom. 4:1—5:2; Gal. 2:15–16, 21; Eph. 2:8–9). As paganism came into the church, the heathen concept that human works are essential for salvation was added to the gospel. As a result, the only way of salvation became hidden from huge masses of people for centuries. Thus, while Satan was leading the organized church into apostasy, he also was changing the message that it was to preach so that members of his kingdom could not be transferred into the kingdom of God.

Satan realized that, if he were to keep the organized church apostate and the gospel hidden, he had to pervert the interpretation of Scripture and even prevent the study of the Bible if possible. In 230 A.D. Origen, a church leader who had been influenced greatly by pagan philosophy, published a work in which he developed an allegorical method of interpreting the Scriptures.[18] Instead of giving the words of the Bible their common, ordinary meaning, this method searched for symbolic, hidden meanings. It distorted the meaning intended by the writer into what the interpreter wanted to find in the Bible.[19] Because of Origen's position and influence, this method strongly affected the organized church.

As the church became more pagan, it had to look for support outside the Scriptures to justify its apostate teachings. So eventually it departed from the view that the Bible is to be the church's sole source of authority for faith and practice. It placed church tradition on a level of equal authority with the Bible and through time asserted that the church is the ultimate source of authority.[20] Finally, it forbade the laity to read the Scriptures and strongly opposed the translation of the Bible into the languages of the common people.[21]

Because he hated the teaching concerning the future, political, theocratic kingdom, Satan was determined to obliterate it from the belief of the church. In the East the concept of the future kingdom was "inseparably bound up with the Christian faith down to the middle of the second century."[22] But by the close of the second century, church leaders in Alexandria, Egypt, began to attack the concept. Having been influenced by the pagan philosophical concept that anything physical is evil, they rejected the idea of a future kingdom with physical blessings as being too carnal and sensual.[23] Origen's allegorical method of interpretation helped to advance this rejection.[24]

In addition, a strong anti-Semitic spirit developed in the Eastern church. Gentiles who professed to be Christians increasingly developed a strong bias against anything Jewish. Because the premillennial belief in the earthly, political kingdom-rule of Messiah in the future was the same hope that had motivated the Jewish people for centuries, that belief was increasingly "stigmatized as 'Jewish' and consequently 'heretical'" by Eastern Gentile Christians.[25] As a result, Premillennialism was discredited through guilt by association.

In the West, belief in the future, theocratic kingdom was still a point of orthodoxy in the fourth century.[26] It began to disappear there at the same time that the church became united with the state and began to go apostate.[27] The writings of Augustine (A.D. 354–430), the most influential ancient church leader in the West, caused most of the organized church to reject the belief in the coming kingdom.[28] In *City of God* Augustine taught that God's promised kingdom is present on earth now in this present age, the organized church is that kingdom, Satan is bound now, eventually the church will conquer the world, and the kingdom age will end at the Second Coming when the history of this world will end.[29, 30]

Augustine rejected the idea of a future kingdom for the same reason as the Alexandrian leaders.[31] In addition, with the church having become the exclusive religion of the empire, it did appear that it was conquering the world.[32] In order to hold to his position, Augustine used Origen's allegorical method to interpret Old Testament prophecies about the kingdom.[33] Augustine's view led the Church of Rome to conceive of itself "as the universal church destined to bring all within its fold."[34]

The development of the strong anti-Semitic spirit and the teaching that the organized church is the future Messianic Kingdom foretold by God through the Old Testament prophets were part of a concept of replacement. According to that concept, since Israel as a nation rejected Jesus Christ as its Messiah during His First Coming, God rejected that nation forever as His people. This theology claims that God has no future program for Israel and that He replaced Israel with the church as His people. Thus the church became the "Israel of God" and inherits the blessings promised to national Israel. This concept violated and contradicted the Scriptures (Gen 13:14–15; 15:18; 17:7–8, 19; 1 Sam. 12:22; 2 Sam. 7:23–24; Jer. 30:11; Rom. 11:28–29).[35]

As a result of the inroads of paganism, the perversion of the gospel, the abuse and neglect of the Scriptures, the rejection of the theocratic-kingdom concept, and the replacement-of-Israel view, the organized church of the Middle Ages departed drastically from what God had intended it to be. Because of its apostate condition, the church instigated such things as the military crusades against other professing Christians, Jewish people, and Muslims and brought the Inquisition to bear against people who disagreed with it.[36] Satan used the church of the Middle Ages as a tool to bring dishonor to God and His kingdom.

The Threat of Islam

Although the church had moved into apostasy after the fourth century, it still retained certain elements of divine truth, such as the deity of Christ. It also was very careful to preserve copies of the Scriptures, even though it did abuse their interpretation and study. As long as any Christian truth and the Scriptures continued to exist, Satan could not rest. He felt it imperative to rid the world of these elements of the universal kingdom of God.

Satan attempted to accomplish his goal through the rise of a new religion in Arabia. Muhammad began his career as the founder of Islam in A.D. 610.[37] By the time of his death in A.D. 632, he had converted all of Arabia to his faith.[38] During the next one hundred years, his followers conquered the Holy Land and Syria, most of the eastern Roman Empire, all lands eastward to India, Egypt, all of North Africa, and large areas of Spain.[39] In much of this conquered territory the church dwindled and died because of its apostate condition.

The forces of Islam threatened to conquer all of Europe, thereby converting it into a Muslim continent. God countered this threat, however, when the Franks and other European tribes, under the leadership of Charles Martel, defeated the Muslims at the Battle of Tours in A.D. 732.[40] Thus the Church, the Scriptures, and such truths as the deity of Christ were saved from possible extinction.

The Divine Counteraction of Church Apostasy

From the time that the organized church began to go apostate to the time of the Reformation, God preserved a small remnant of people who opposed the apostate church. Here and there throughout Europe were groups of people who repudiated the authority of the Roman Church and its pope and rejected its pagan beliefs and practices. They held to the true gospel, regarded the Scriptures as their source of authority, encouraged the study of the Bible by laypeople, observed the Lord's Supper as a memorial rather than a sacrifice, and had pastors instead of priests. Many of these groups believed in the future, political, theocratic kingdom.[41] Some, such as the Waldensians, sent out lay evangelists to preach the gospel to the members of Satan's kingdom. Satan could not tolerate such true, biblical faith and witness. Therefore, he prompted the organized church to persecute these groups severely. Special crusades and the Inquisition were used against them. Some groups were annihilated. Many people were tortured, executed, or driven from their homes and countries, to be hunted like fugitives.[42]

Toward the end of the Middle Ages God raised up several men who began calling for reform within the organized church. Among the most prominent of these were John Wycliffe of England

(1324–1384), John Huss of Bohemia (1369–1415) and Jerome Savonarola of Florence, Italy (1452–1498). Wycliffe opposed monasticism, the authority of the Roman Church and pope, the idea that the Lord's Supper is a sacrifice, and the corruption of the priesthood. He urged that the church reform itself to New Testament standards. He was instrumental in producing the first Bible in the English language, and he sent out lay preachers called Lollards. These were persecuted and finally extinguished.[43]

As a result of reading Wycliffe's writings, Huss began proclaiming the same evangelical concepts in Bohemia. His views caused so much trouble for the Roman Church that the pope excommunicated him and ordered him to appear before the Church Council of Constance. At first Huss refused to go, but he finally consented when the emperor promised him safe conduct. At the council he was condemned and burned at the stake in spite of the emperor's guarantee. The church claimed that faith did not have to be kept with heretics.[44]

Savonarola was a fiery preacher of reform who attacked corruption in government, society, and the church. On one occasion he even wrote that the pope was not a Christian. He was excommunicated, imprisoned, hanged to death, and burned by order of the church.[45] Thus Satan tried to squelch these attempts to reform the church to God's standards.

The Renaissance

Between 1350 and 1650 Europe experienced a great cultural change that marked the transition from medieval to modern times.[46] A new interest in the classic literature and art of Greece and Rome and in science was aroused. This new awakening has been called the Renaissance.

Satan attempted to use the Renaissance as his instrument for turning the thoughts of man away from God altogether. In southern Europe the movement developed into a secular, skeptical humanism with man, rather than God, being the focus of attention. People did continue to observe the formal ritual of the church, but "the tendency was to forget the claims of God upon the individual in daily life."[47] Even the popes of the time were more interested in culture than in spiritual things.[48]

God was determined to use the Renaissance as His tool to prepare Europe for the coming Reformation. Thus in northern Europe the movement developed into a religious humanism. There scholars became more interested in the Judeo-Christian past than in the classical past. "They were more interested in man as a human being with a soul than they were in him as a rational creature."[49] They studied biblical manuscripts in the original languages, applied the humanistic techniques to the study of the Scriptures, reemphasized the historical-grammatical interpretation as opposed to the allegorical, produced grammars and dictionaries of the biblical languages, and printed the Greek New Testament. The invention of printing by movable type in 1455 made the printing and distribution of the Scriptures and the writings of reformers easier, quicker, and less costly.[50] All of this made it possible for men to see how drastically the church of their day had changed from the Church of the New Testament.[51]

During the time of the Renaissance, a strong middle class and a spirit of nationalism developed. God used these also to prepare Europe for the Reformation. People were beginning to resent the fact that a foreign pope ruled their national churches, appointed their church leaders, demanded a tax to support him and to build ornate churches in Rome, exempted his clergy from their national laws and courts, and dictated political policies to their governments.[52]

The Reformation

God's greatest counteraction of the apostasy in the organized church was a new spiritual movement known as the Reformation. This movement developed in several stages. It began in Germany in 1517 when Martin Luther, a monk and professor of the Roman Church, started to write and speak against the wrong beliefs and practices of the church. Luther called for reform, but the church refused to heed the call. It condemned and excommunicated Luther and demanded that he be delivered for trial and punishment. With the new wave of nationalistic spirit, the princes of northern Germany supported and protected Luther. Thus the Lutheran Church was able to be formed. When the Diet of Spires (1529) condemned Lutheran doctrine and made rulings against Lutheranism, the northern princes registered a formal protest. From that time on they and all others who called for the apostate church to reform were called Protestants.[53]

While the Reformation was beginning in Germany, it also was springing up in Switzerland. Under the leadership of Ulric Zwingli, the canton of Zurich established the Reformed Church. The Presbyterian Church was started in Geneva through the work of John Calvin.[54] The Anabaptist movement came into existence and grew in Germany and Switzerland under such men as Grebel, Manz, and Hubmaier.[55]

Denmark, Sweden, and Norway adopted the Lutheran faith.[56] In France groups of people adopted Protestantism and became known as Huguenots.[57] In northern Netherlands most people accepted the Reformed faith, while a good-sized minority became Anabaptist in belief but called themselves Mennonites.[58] Under the fiery preaching of John Knox, Scotland accepted the Reformed faith.[59] The Reformation also began in England when Henry VIII broke the English Church away from Rome.[60]

The Protestant Reformation emphasized three New Testament truths. The first was justification by faith alone. The pagan concept of human works for salvation was rejected, and the original, pure gospel was declared once again. The second was the priesthood of the believer. The Reformers did away with the Roman Church's wide cleavage between clergy and laity. It stressed the New Testament concept that every Christian is a priest before God and thereby has the privilege of ministering and of studying the Bible on his own. The third was the concept that the Bible, not the church, is the final authority for faith and practice.[61]

6

THE CONFLICT
FROM THE COUNTER REFORMATION
THROUGH THE PHILOSOPHY OF RITSCHL

The Counter Reformation

WITH THE RISE AND WIDESPREAD growth of Protestantism, Satan was confronted with a twofold task. First, it was imperative that he prevent the entire organized church from going Protestant. Second, it was essential that he get rid of Protestantism, since it had rejected much of the apostasy and was preaching the true gospel. In order to accomplish his task, Satan used a new wave of religious fervor that began to energize the Roman Church in response to the Reformation. This revitalization of the Roman Church became known as the Counter Reformation.

One important phase of the Counter Reformation was the Council of Trent which met from 1545 to 1563. Although this council did adopt some healthy reforms, it reasserted the Roman Church's continued belief in many of its traditional doctrines, such as the following: justification is by faith plus subsequent works, the seven sacraments are channels of grace, the Lord's Supper is a sacrifice, and the tradition of the church is of equal authority with the Scriptures. For the first time the church declared the apocryphal books to be canonical and of equal authority with the Bible. The council turned the Roman

Church's beliefs into a dogma that was binding upon all its people.[1] Thus Satan succeeded in preventing the entire Roman Church from returning to New Testament principles.

The Counter Reformation gave birth to the Jesuits, a monastic order devoted to fighting Protestantism and spreading the Roman faith. Although they frequently used unethical means, the Jesuits were able to regain Poland, southern Netherlands, and large parts of Germany for the Roman Church. Their missionaries spread their faith to several new lands.[2]

The Roman Church instituted the Index, a list of books its people were forbidden to read. The Index kept many of the church's members from reading Protestant literature.[3] Thus Satan was able to prevent these people from becoming exposed to New Testament teaching.

Finally, the Counter Reformation employed persecution in its fight against Protestantism. Governments controlled by the Roman Church were prompted to annihilate the Reformation faith. The Spanish government led in this activity in behalf of the church. It established the Inquisition both in Spain and the Netherlands. Multitudes of people were tortured and burned. Many were forced to recant their Protestant views. In the Netherlands the Spanish troops instituted a reign of terror that executed at least seventeen thousand.[4]

In France the government persecuted the Huguenots fiercely from 1538 to 1559, then conducted eight bloody wars against them from 1559 to 1598. In the St. Bartholomew's Day Massacre in 1572 some ten to twenty thousand Protestants were butchered for their faith.[5]

In England Queen Mary Tudor (1553–1558) executed some three hundred Protestant pastors and forced the rest to flee the country.[6] When Queen Elizabeth I restored a moderate form of Protestantism to the land, the pope began training Jesuits to conduct guerrilla warfare in England. He also persuaded the king of Spain to conquer England for the Roman Church by sailing the great "invincible" Spanish Armada against her.[7] The Armada sailed in 1588, but she suffered a very embarrassing defeat as a result of good English seamanship, contrary weather, and other circumstances beyond human control.[8] Thus God destroyed the naval power of the Roman Church's most powerful ally and established England as the champion of Protestantism in Europe.[9] This defeat aided the cause of Protestantism not only in England, but also in the Netherlands, where it limited Spanish power.[10]

By 1609 much of Europe was divided into two armed camps of Protestantism and Romanism. For political as well as religious reasons these two camps waged the Thirty Years' War against each other (1618–1648). Finally, when the war was settled by the Peace of Westphalia, Lutheranism and Calvinism became recognized religions, and the boundaries of Protestant and Roman Church states were fixed.[11] This ended the Reformation Era and the systematic persecution of the Protestant movement by the Roman Church. God had preserved Protestantism from external destruction.

Internal Attacks Against Protestantism

While Satan was attempting to destroy the Protestant witness of the gospel through outside forces, he also was working to disgrace and destroy the movement from within. Although all the Protestant groups had rejected much of the apostasy of the Roman Church, many still carried with them some of the Roman beliefs and practices. Most groups continued to reject the concept of a future, theocratic kingdom. They believed that their church was the kingdom of God on earth and that it was to operate basically as Israel had in Old Testament times. This meant that the Protestant Church and the state were to be united, with the state enforcing the church's policies. No one was to be permitted to hold beliefs contrary to the official teaching of the church. These concepts were contrary to Scripture. Because of these wrong beliefs, some Protestant groups resorted to the same tactic as the Roman Church—the bloody persecution of those who held other beliefs.[12] Through this means Satan brought disgrace to the Protestant movement.

The Anabaptists disagreed strongly with the policy of persecuting those of contrary belief. They were convinced that church and state should be kept separate and that no one church should enforce its beliefs upon others. One reason for this conviction was the fact that many Anabaptists rejected the idea that the church is the kingdom promised in the Old Testament. They believed in a future, theocratic kingdom on earth.

Satan attempted to stamp out this belief in the future kingdom by trying to destroy the Anabaptist movement. Because the Anabaptists disagreed with certain views of the other Protestants, they were persecuted severely.[13] Thus Satan used Protestants to attack other parts of the Reformation faith. Although many Anabaptists were put to death, God continued to preserve the movement.

Since he could not destroy those who taught the doctrine of a future kingdom, Satan tried to disgrace the doctrine. He used a group of fanatical Anabaptists at Munster, Germany, who introduced to the concept of the kingdom extreme ideas and practices contrary to Scripture. Their radical practices not only disgraced belief in a future kingdom, but also brought further persecution from Protestants and Roman Catholics.[14]

The Apostasy of the Modern Era
The Rise of Rationalism and Empiricism

Satan had not been able to destroy Protestantism, but he still was determined to rid the world of the true gospel; the belief that the Bible was God's inspired revelation to man; and the hope of God establishing His future, theocratic kingdom with all its blessings for man. With this goal in view he prompted the rise of some new movements that would trigger a chain reaction of apostasy. This apostasy would affect the whole world, including much of Protestantism.

During the late seventeenth and eighteenth centuries a new intellectual movement known as rationalism developed in Europe.[15] The rationalists stressed the importance of human reason and the senses, as opposed to divine revelation, as the key to discovering truth. Men began to look at the universe as a machine that operates solely by natural law, not by divine providence or intervention. As the knowledge of non-Christian religions grew, some thinkers began searching for a natural religion that would be common to all men apart from the Bible and the Church.[16] The rise of rationalism was accompanied by the introduction of empiricism. Empiricists believed that no idea should be adopted unless its truth has been established through repeated tests that can be observed by the human senses.[17] In other words, it is reasonable to believe only those things that can be demonstrated through the scientific method. When carried to its logical conclusion, empiricism ruled out belief in truths that came by divine revelation. Such truths deal with spiritual things, and spiritual things are not subject to scientific tests that can be observed by the senses.

The Development of Deism

Rationalism and empiricism gave birth to a new religion called deism. This new faith began in England during the seventeenth century, then spread to France, Germany, and America in the eighteenth. It could be called a natural religion or religion of reason.[18] Deism accepted the rationalistic concept that the universe is governed solely by natural law apart from divine providence or intervention, but it could not explain the origin of the universe apart from God. Thus one of its major teachings was as follows: a Supreme Being created the universe; but after He created it, He totally withdrew Himself from it and had nothing more to do with it.[19]

This major concept led deism to several conclusions. First, there has been no supernatural revelation of truth to man since the world began. Second, there is no such thing as miracles. Third, the Bible is not a supernaturally inspired book. Fourth, Jesus Christ was not God incarnate in human flesh.[20] Deism had to draw these conclusions in order to avoid the idea that God has been active in human history.

Another major teaching of deism was this: since there has been no supernatural revelation, man's only means of discovering truth is through human reason by use of the scientific method. Deism practically ignored the problem of human sin. It believed that man was essentially good and perfectible; therefore, it expected continued progress to a more perfect order on earth.[21] In other words, deism believed that man would establish an earthly utopia through his own efforts, without the supernatural intervention of God. This new faith proved to be an ancestor of liberal Protestantism.[22]

The Divine Counteraction of Rationalism, Empiricism, and Deism

Through rationalism, empiricism, and deism, Satan was striking blows at the gospel, the Bible, and the concept of a future theocratic kingdom. God countered these movements in order to preserve a continuing witness for the kingdom of God. The counteraction in Germany was in the form of the pietist movement of the seventeenth and eighteenth centuries. People of established churches began to gather together for Bible study and prayer and to emphasize a life of piety. Pietism gave birth to the Moravian Church, which, in its warm evangelical zeal, sent out missionaries to preach the gospel.[23]

The counteraction in England was the eighteenth century Wesleyan revivals, which reached millions with the gospel, gave birth to the Methodist Church, and saved England from national disaster.[24] In America God used the Great Awakening, which evangelized multitudes through such men as George Whitefield and Jonathan Edwards.[25]

The Philosophies of Kant, Hegel, and Schleiermacher

During the late eighteenth and nineteenth centuries, Satan began to build a superstructure upon the foundation of modern apostasy laid through rationalism, empiricism, and deism. The original building materials used in this superstructure were the philosophies of Immanuel Kant, George Hegel, and Fredrich Schleiermacher.

Kant (1724–1804) declared that knowledge is limited to the world that the human senses can perceive. Since man can know only what his senses experience, there can be no knowledge that comes through special, divine revelation.[26] In fact, there is no such thing as special revelation. Religious beliefs can be based only upon the universal concept of duty or law that all men possess.[27] In other words, man's concept of God and spiritual things must be derived from his daily, moral experience.[28] Kant's philosophy ruled out the belief that the Scriptures are God's special revelation to man.

Hegel, who died in 1831, concluded that the true essence of Christianity resides in its great ideas, not in the historical events that gave birth to them. Indeed, whether or not the ideas are based upon true historical facts is unimportant. Thus, although the ideas of Christianity are derived from the Bible, their truth is not dependent upon the historical accuracy of that book.[29] Thus, according to Hegel, an inerrant Bible is not essential to true Christianity.

Schleiermacher (1758–1834) proposed that, at its heart, true religion is neither belief in nor obedience to a system of theology or a code of moral absolutes. Instead, religion is "an immediately experienced relation to God."[30] Thus doctrine and standards of conduct are not important. What is important is experience. The Bible is not a divinely inspired book of instruction. Instead, it is a human interpretation of man's religious experience. Thus, according to Schleiermacher, the Scriptures are not the final authority for faith and practice. Only living religious experience is the final authority.[31]

The Development of Destructive Criticism

These new philosophies of religious authority and of the meaning of revelation made possible the development of destructive criticism of the Bible.[32] This movement appeared at the time Schleiermacher was completing his work.[33] Protestant scholars began to abandon the belief that the Bible is a divinely inspired, infallible, inerrant record of divine revelation to man.[34] They substituted the idea that the Scriptures are a human record of the development of man's religious consciousness.[35] Thus, although they possess some records of historical value, the Scriptures contain widely differing concepts of God and His will for man. They also contain legends, fiction, errors, and contradictions.[36]

Scholars began to evaluate the Bible like any other piece of literature.[37] They questioned the reliability of the Old Testament, especially
its record of creation, the flood, and the development of Israel.[38] Some
concluded that the Gospels did not always present an accurate record
of the true Jesus of history; therefore, it was necessary "to distinguish
the words and character of Jesus from the interpretations which the
church had later placed upon Him and His work."[39] Predictive
prophecy and miracles were rejected as unauthentic, and the teaching
about the future theocratic kingdom was either rejected or interpreted
in terms of nineteenth-century thought.[40]

Thus Satan, knowing that the account of his rebellion and
defeat is presented in the Bible, was trying desperately to dis-
credit that book. He directed his attack especially against those
portions of Scripture that record the origin of himself and man,
the first promise of his fall and the Redeemer, the prophecies of
his defeat and the establishment of the theocratic kingdom, and
the miraculous powers that the Redeemer possesses to destroy
his kingdom and establish God's.[41]

The Rise of Commercialism

With science giving birth to many new discoveries and inven-
tions, and with the Industrial Revolution providing the means
for mass production of goods, man was faced with the glowing
prospect of an unprecedented abundance of material things.
Numerous people made mammon their god and materialism
their philosophy of life. Satan used commercialism as a tool for
getting man so absorbed with temporal things that he had no
time to think about God or his own destiny after this life.[42]

The Birth of Communism

Along with its promise of material benefits, commercialism
brought some grave injustices. Working people often were
exploited, as their employers made themselves wealthy at their
expense. The situation became so severe that it was only a matter of time until someone would cry for a revolution to change

the social order. That time came when Karl Marx published his Communist Manifesto (1848) and *Das Kapital* (1867). Marx believed that history is controlled by economic factors and is characterized by continual class conflict. Thus everything is either a direct or indirect result of the economic struggle between workers and capitalists. Even religion is a product of economic forces.[43] Capitalists use its concept of punishment and reward in the hereafter as their means of persuading the workers to accept quietly their exploited status in the present life. Thus religion is the "opiate of the people."[44] In the class struggle, religion should be annihilated.

Because of these Marxist ideas, Communism waged war against the Bible, the organized church, belief in the existence of God and life hereafter, and the concepts of human sin and divinely revealed moral absolutes.[45] In place of these it substituted materialistic atheism and the hope of a future, man-made utopia on earth. This utopia would be a communistic society in which every man produces according to his ability and shares in the goods of society according to his needs.[46] Thus, in communism Satan not only had an enemy of Christianity but also a counterfeit hope to substitute for belief in the future theocratic kingdom.[47]

The Impact of the Evolutionary Theory

The publication of Darwin's *Origin of Species* in 1859 shook the scientific and religious worlds. In his work Darwin offered evidence for the gradual evolution of living things from simpler to more complex forms, gave a reasonable explanation as to how evolution takes place—through the process of natural selection or survival of the fittest—and used his theory "to account for the origin of the human race."[48]

Through time the theory of evolution was applied to religion as well as biology. The impact of this application upon Christianity was earthshaking. First, by asserting that man evolved from lower forms of life, it struck at the biblical view that man originated by a direct, special, creative act of God.[49] Second, by setting back the date of man's origin by aeons of time, it raised doubts about the centrality of the Judaeo-Christian influence in the history of mankind.[50] Third, by questioning the biblical account of the fall of man, it caused a new definition of sin. To evolution sin is merely the remnant of animal instinct in man.[51] Fourth, this new concept of sin led to new views concerning redemption. There was no need of a redeemer dying as a substitute to pay the penalty of man's sin. Thus Jesus Christ was not the Redeemer making vicarious atonement.[52] Redemption is the gradual process of educating man to overcome his animal instincts.[53]

Fifth, evolution portrayed Christianity, the Bible, and the concept of one God as being products of the evolutionary development of man's religious consciousness.[54] Thus the relationship of Christianity to non-Christian religions is not that of absolute truth as opposed to error. Instead, the various religions represent different stages in the development of man's religious insight, with Christianity being the most advanced stage thus far.[55] Sixth, with religion being in a continual state of development, there can be no such thing as moral absolutes that are binding upon all men at all times. "Good conduct is merely those actions deemed suitable by each generation for the conduct of society."[56]

Evolution caused two different mental attitudes among those who accepted it as being true. One attitude was that of despair. Some people found it impossible to reconcile the horrible "red in tooth and claw" struggle and waste of the evolutionary process with the existence of a good and sovereign Creator.[57] This destroyed their belief in God. Everything appeared to exist and operate purely by chance. They concluded that there is no intelligent purpose for life and the existence of man.[58] A modern-day evolutionist who came to this conclusion expressed it this way:

> Man is the result of a purposeless and materialistic process that did not have him in mind. He was not planned. He is a state of matter, a form of life, a sort of animal, and a species of the Order Primates, akin nearly or remotely to all of life and indeed to all that is material.[59]

For many nineteenth-century Protestants, evolution caused an attitude of optimism. They concluded that evolution is the process that God used to create and to maintain life. Thus God works within natural processes instead of by miraculous intervention in the natural order. This view stressed the immanence of God—the idea that He is everywhere present in nature.[60] It rejected the biblical concept of a perfect order coming through the direct intervention of God in the establishment of His future, theocratic kingdom. It substituted the idea that the world would become increasingly better through human effort.[61] In evolution Satan had a powerful tool with which to attack Christianity in many different areas.

The Divine Counteraction During the Nineteenth Century

While Satan was assaulting the kingdom of God with faulty philosophies, destructive criticism, commercialism, communistic ideas, and evolution, God was countering his attacks with an active witness of His own. The nineteenth century was a time of unprecedented Protestant missionary activity. Mission boards were founded both in England and America. The gospel was carried to India, Africa, China, and other lands by such pioneers as William Carey, David Livingstone, and Adoniram Judson.[62] America experienced the Second Awakening and numerous frontier revivals during the earlier part of the century.[63] As some schools became apostate, God raised up new ones, such as Andover and Princeton Seminaries, to train men in the true faith.[64] Over the course of the century great evangelistic efforts were put forth by such men as Charles Finney, Dwight L. Moody, and R. A. Torrey.[65] Through all of this many souls were added to the kingdom of God.

The Philosophy of Ritschl

During the latter half of the nineteenth century the philosophy of Albrecht Ritschl began to affect Protestant thinking. Ritschl (1822–1889) agreed with Schleiermacher that all religious belief is grounded in religious experience, but he also agreed with Kant that religious experience is essentially moral in nature.[66] Thus

Christianity is not doctrine; instead, it is totally the daily practice of life.[67]

Ritschl emphasized the love of God so much that he suppressed the concepts of God's holiness and justice and denied divine wrath. This caused him to reject the idea of original sin and the doctrine of the punishment of the lost.[68] According to Ritschl, the kingdom of God is "the organization of humanity through action inspired by love."[69] He believed that the goal of religion is the victory of man over his bondage to nature.[70] Ritschl's philosophy helped to develop the social gospel.[71]

THE CONFLICT FROM LIBERAL PROTESTANTISM THROUGH THE DENIAL OF A PERSONAL GOD

Further Apostasy of the Modern Era
The Principles of Liberal Protestantism

THROUGH THE COMBINED INFLUENCE of the philosophies and movements of the nineteenth century, Satan succeeded in getting much of Protestantism to go apostate. Liberal Protestantism developed during the latter part of the century and reached its peak in the early decades of the twentieth century.[1] Its development could be described as a Protestant response and adjustment to nineteenth-century trends in scientific, philosophical, economic, and political thought.[2] The liberals thought it was necessary to reinterpret the gospel to be able to present it in the thought forms of the modern world.[3]

Several principles became characteristic of most of liberal Protestantism. First, there was a spirit of open-mindedness and tolerance toward new modes of thought and toward other groups within Christendom. Theological and denominational differences were considered insignificant.[4] Second, there was confidence in the scientific method as a means to truth not only in the study of the material world, but also in the realm of Biblical criticism and the history of religion.[5] Third, a strong feeling against theological dogmatism developed. Men became skeptical about the possibility of obtaining sure knowledge of ultimate reality.[6] Fourth, there was a desire to emphasize similarities rather than differences. Liberals began to look for the common features of Christianity and non-Christian religions. They stressed the immanence of God so as to eliminate the differences between the supernatural and the natural and between God and man.[7]

Fifth, liberal Protestantism expressed great confidence in man and his future. It believed that man and his society were perfectible.[8] Sixth, it stressed the authority of individual, religious experience as opposed to Biblical or church authority.[9] Seventh, it made the example and ethical teachings of Jesus Christ central to everything.[10] Eighth, it criticized many of the traditional beliefs of Protestantism. Many things formerly believed were now regarded as unessential to Christianity. Belief had to be accommodated to new knowledge and ways.[11] Ninth, liberalism became permeated with social idealism. It concluded that the church is responsible for righting social wrongs and for bringing the social structure into conformity with the ideal of the kingdom of God on earth.[12]

Liberal Protestantism developed a theology that would agree with its basic principles. In its doctrine of God it stressed the immanence of God so strongly that it practically assumed a unity of God and the world. It erased the clear distinction between the infinite, perfect God and the finite, corrupt world. It stated that God is present in all the processes of nature.[13]

This emphasis upon the immanence of God colored almost all the rest of liberal theology. It disposed of belief in miracles and the distinction between the supernatural and the natural.[14] In the doctrine of man, it implied that man has a spark of divinity within him. Thus there was no fall of man or inherited guilt; man is essentially good.[15] In the doctrine of the church, it denied the sharp distinction between the Church and the world; thus, it de-emphasized the importance of the organized church.[16] Concerning eschatology, it rejected the concept of eternal punishment and stressed the fulfillment of life now rather than the hereafter.[17] With regard to revelation, the notion that God is in everything led to the conclusion that He can be known in every experience.[18]

Concerning the doctrine of Christ, it implied that Jesus was only a man, being subject even to error. However, as a man, Jesus raised humanity to its highest level by allowing God to be supremely immanent in Him. He was not the kind of Redeemer that Paul and the Church pictured. Instead, He was the great Teacher of ethics who gave the greatest example of how man can allow God to become supremely immanent in him.[19] In the matter of salvation, the idea of immanence ruled out the concept of God entering a person's life in an instantaneous moment of conversion. The liberals concluded that, since every person is born with God in him, conversion is simply a matter of educating a child to act like Christ.[20] Finally, in the area of religious authority, liberalism says that, because God is immanent in each person, the final court of appeal for faith and practice is the individual's own reason, conscience, and intuition. Nothing is authoritative for an individual unless it is meaningful to him personally.[21] In essence, this means that each person is his own authority, and that there are no absolutes of faith and conduct to which all men are responsible.

Development of the Social Gospel

Although commercialism had produced many social injustices, there was a great air of optimism that arose in society during the last quarter of the nineteenth century. It reached its peak in the years before World War I.[22] The amazing accomplishments of science, the concept of evolutionary progress, and the liberal Protestant ideas of the perfectibility of man and of God working immanently in the world all contributed to the belief that the transformation of society was possible.[23] Men began to preach the message of social change so extensively that eventually their message became known as the social gospel.

Liberal Protestant advocates of the social gospel declared that the church should be concerned primarily with this world.[24] It should divert its efforts from the salvation of individuals to the salvation of society.[25] The church should bring in the kingdom of God on earth instead of teaching about a future, theocratic kingdom to be established in Person by Jesus Christ.[26] It can do this by reconstructing the entire social order in accord with the ethical teachings of Jesus.[27]

In its theology the social-gospel movement emphasized the immanence of God as the basis of social oneness. It concluded that, since God is immanent in all men, He is the Father of all, and all men are brothers.[28] Christ's redeeming work was regarded as the battle against religious bigotry, graft, political power, injustice, mob action, militarism, and class contempt.[29] The church was to save the world, not be saved out of it. Thus Satan was able to pervert the true gospel again and to turn much of Protestantism away from preaching it.

The Divine Counteraction of Liberal Protestantism

While liberalism and the social gospel were permeating Protestantism, God was preventing total apostasy by maintaining His witness in the world. He did this through various means. In addition to reaching the unsaved through the evangelistic campaigns of Dwight L. Moody, R.A. Torrey, and Billy Sunday, He fortified believers through the establishment of Bible and prophetic conferences at numerous places.[30] These conferences helped to ground Christians in the basic doctrines of Christianity and to confirm their hope in the Second Coming of Christ to establish the theocratic kingdom.

As many Christian schools yielded to the liberal apostasy, God raised up new schools to take their place in the task of giving sound, Christian instruction. One interesting aspect of this phase of the counteraction was the rise of the Bible school movement. From the 1880s through the early decades of the twentieth century numerous Bible schools were founded in such cities as New York, Chicago, Boston, Los Angeles, and Philadelphia. New Christian liberal arts colleges and seminaries also were begun.[31]

In 1909 two Christian laymen financed the publication of a set of volumes that defended the basic beliefs of biblical Christianity against the apostasy of the day. The set was called *The Fundamentals*, and hundreds of thousands of copies were sent to church leaders all over the world. Because of the title of these volumes, those people who held to the doctrines defended therein came to be called fundamentalists.[32] The publication in 1909 of the Scofield Reference Bible, with its explanatory notes, aided laypeople in their understanding of the Scriptures and emphasized the hope of the future, theocratic kingdom. From 1918 to 1931 the fundamentalists challenged the growing liberal control of several of the major Protestant denominations. This led to the Modernist-Fundamentalist controversies within various church groups.[33] As the leadership of various denominations surrendered to liberalism, many fundamentalists withdrew from those organizations and began new denominational and interdenominational groups.

The Birth of the Ecumenical Movement

The latter nineteenth and early twentieth centuries witnessed the birth of a movement toward unity within Protestantism. This movement was prompted by several factors. First, many people were disturbed over the contrast between biblical statements about Christian unity and the divided state of Protestantism.[34] Second, liberalism de-emphasized the importance of theology.[35] Third, there was the desire to end the confusion and duplication of efforts caused by church divisions on the mission field.[36] Fourth, the social-gospel advocates wanted Christendom to give a united expression of concern about the ethical and social issues of the modern world.[37] Fifth, through various youth and student movements young people expressed their impatience with the differences that divided Christendom.[38]

In response to these factors the Federal Council of Churches was formed in 1908 in America to provide a central organ for united Protestant action on social problems, afford opportunity for the denominations to understand each other better through calm discussion of their differences, and facilitate cooperation on the mission field.[39] At first the emphasis was upon interdenominational cooperation on a worldwide scale, rather than upon the organizational merger of all bodies into one.[40]

The Development of Neoorthodoxy

The great scope and horrors of World War I severely crippled the social-gospel concept of the gradual perfecting of man and society. The optimism of liberal Protestantism didn't seem to agree with reality.[41] The war had demonstrated the corruption rather than the supposed inherent goodness of man. There was need for a revision of liberal, Protestant theology. Thus, in 1918 a new theological movement began within Protestantism in western Europe.[42] Through time it spread to America and dominated much of Protestant thinking even into the post-World War II era.

This movement began as a severe criticism of the fallacies of liberal theology. It accepted some concepts from existentialism, a nineteenth-century movement that had been critical of liberal theology and the institutional church.[43] In its theology the new movement stressed the sovereignty, transcendence, wrath, and judgment of God, as well as His mercy and love. God is infinitely above and supreme over the world. This emphasis was opposed to the liberal concept of the immanence of God.[44] The new movement also emphasized that Christ was more than just a man; He was God come to man—truly God and truly man.[45] It also stressed the sinfulness of man and of every human movement, and indicated that sin is so deeply rooted in man that only a redeeming act of God can overcome it.[46] It stated that the final authority for faith and practice is not religious experience.[47] It concluded that, although the church is obligated to speak about social evils, the social order cannot be transformed progressively into the kingdom of God on earth.[48] These theological statements sounded so much like orthodoxy that eventually the movement became known as the new orthodoxy, or neoorthodoxy.

Although neoorthodoxy frequently used the language of orthodoxy, it often gave the language unorthodox meanings. In several crucial areas it differed with orthodox, biblical Christianity altogether. In the area of God's revelation to man, neoorthodoxy declared that the final authority for faith and practice is not the Bible. In fact, God never has given divine revelation through declared statements of truth, whether spoken or written.

According to neoorthodoxy, the final authority is the revelation of Himself that God gives to an individual when He encounters him personally.[49] This means that no divine revelation is the same for all men. God may reveal one thing to one man, but something else to another. The Word of God to an individual is whatever God used to speak to that individual personally. Thus, if God speaks to a person through a passage of the Bible then that passage *becomes* the Word of God for that person. But if God never speaks to a person through the Bible, then the Bible never is the Word of God for him.[50] This view also means that, even if a man wanted to learn something about God through nature, he could not do so unless God spoke to him personally through some aspect of nature. In essence, neoorthodoxy believed that there is no objective revelation of God in the Bible or nature.

Neoorthodoxy differed from orthodox Christianity in other ways. It believed that the original Scriptures contained error. It held that the biblical accounts of creation, the Fall of Man, and the last judgment are not referring to actual historical events. Instead, these accounts are myths or symbolic ways of presenting important truths that could not be expressed in any other way.[51] Actually, the Fall was not a once-for-all, past event; it is the turning away from God that is true of every human life and action.[52] Neoorthodoxy stated that the kingdom of God will be established by God, not man, but that its establishment is beyond history. The biblical idea of the future, theocratic kingdom is a symbol. Its purpose is to picture a divine purpose for history. It is God's way of promising a final victory over evil beyond history.[53]

Thus, although neoorthodoxy opposed numerous liberal tendencies, it also continued several other of those tendencies.[54] The fact that it used biblical language to express unbiblical concepts made some of its teachings an even more deceptive tool than liberalism in Satan's war against the kingdom of God.

The Denial of a Personal God

Satan realized that one of the best ways to establish the permanent, visible form of his kingdom in the world was to prompt man to deny the existence of his archenemy—God. But how could he get man to do this? Throughout history God has used revelation to uncover the reality of His existence to man. In light of this, Satan knew that, in order to accomplish his goal, he must move man to reject all divine revelation. Thus, from the time of rationalism on, he used one philosophy and movement after another to move man in that direction. Rationalism propagated the idea that the world operates purely on a natural basis without the intervention of God; empiricism ruled out belief in truths that come by revelation; deism denied the existence of all forms of special revelation in the world; Kant declared that there can be no knowledge of God through revelation; Hegel raised doubts about the record of God's actions in the world being true, historic fact; Schleiermacher placed the final authority for faith and practice in experience rather than in revelation; destructive criticism rejected the Bible as the infallible, inerrant, supernatural revelation of God to man; commercialism took man's thoughts away from God and spiritual things and focused them on the material things of this life; Communism pictured belief in God as being detrimental to man; evolution in its purest form denied the necessity of a personal God to explain the existence of man and his world; Ritschl placed final authority in experience rather than in revelation; the amazing accomplishments of science gave man confidence that he could solve his own problems apart from God; liberal Protestantism came close to equating God with nature; the social gospel declared that man could establish the kingdom of God on earth without the supernatural intervention of God; and neoorthodoxy taught that there is no objective way that man can learn about God.

Through all of these movements and philosophies Satan kept eating away at the vital organs of man's belief in a personal God by getting man to reject the revelation that God has given. However, until the era of World War I, the disease remained well hidden. Man still had an outer shell of belief intact; therefore, he at least continued to pay lip-service to God, although in actual practice he often acted as if God didn't exist.

As the twentieth century progressed, Satan used one tragic situation after another to chip away more and more of man's outer shell, thereby revealing his growing unbelief in a personal God. The brutalities of modern warfare, as displayed by World War I, the failure of the League of Nations to maintain peace, the economic hardships of the depression of the twenties and thirties, the systematic annihilation of six million Jews by Naziism, the mass death and destruction of World War II, the threat of the annihilation of humanity through a nuclear holocaust, the injustices of racism, the frustrating conflicts of Korea and Vietnam, the hideous assassination of key leaders, the constant friction of the Middle East crisis, the claim of future cataclysmic results of environmental pollution and population explosion, and more examples of genocide progressively drove more and more of humanity to conclude that man is all alone in his predicament. Because man has rejected the biblical testimony that his situation is caused by his own rebellion against God, he has the problem of understanding "human misery, tragedy, and bestiality."[55] Since human suffering does exist, he concludes that it must be because there is no good, personal, sovereign God;[56] or, if there is a God, He has no relevance for the world or mankind. Thus modern man sees all of life and reality on one level—the material; and the cry is made that the idea of a personal God is dead.[57]

Examples of the Denial

From the end of World War I to the end of the twentieth century the denial of God's existence or relevance was expressed in various ways. Secular atheists not only boldly proclaimed their denial of God's existence, but also made attempts to have all public expressions of belief in God banned from society. A prime example was Madalyn Murray O'Hair, whose efforts prompted the United States Supreme Court to abolish Bible reading and prayer in public schools in 1963.

The "God Is Dead" movement of the 1960s was another expression of denial in the United Kingdom and North America. One God-is-dead theologian, Thomas J. J. Altizer, asserted that the world cannot move into the new utopian age until mankind acknowledges that the God of the Bible is dead.[58]

In addition, there were theologians who lectured and wrote about God, but their concept of God was not that of a personal, divine being. For example, Paul Tillich, who taught at Union Theological Seminary (New York), Harvard, and the University of Chicago and was regarded to be one of America's foremost twentieth-century theologians, claimed that God is the impersonal ground or source of all being, not an existing being.[59]

In the late 1970s I heard a radio program in which a philosophy professor was questioned about his view concerning the origin of the universe. The moderator said, "I take it that you do not believe in the existence of a personal creator God."

The philosopher responded, "To the contrary, I believe that there was such a God."

The moderator said, "You put that in the past tense. Do you mean that there was such a God in the past, but that He no longer exists?"

The philosopher said, "Yes, that is what I believe."

The moderator asked, "If there was such a God in the past, but He no longer exists, what happened that caused Him to go out of existence?"

The philosopher responded, "God decided to create the universe through a big bang. But when He caused the big bang, He got too close to it. As a result, it killed Him. Thus He went out of existence when the universe came into existence."

Late in the twentieth century Gerd Ludemann, a German theologian and professor of Early Christianity at Gottingen University, wrote, "With the last of my strength I pushed God himself down into the mire and at last became free. . . . So I prefer from now on to develop a purely human view of religion without having to legitimate myself by a higher authority which theologians call God."[60]

During the twentieth century secular humanists produced and published several humanist manifestoes. In the Humanist Manifesto II, 1973, they stated, "We find insufficient evidence for belief in the existence of a supernatural; it is either meaningless or irrelevant to the survival and fulfillment of the human race. As nontheists, we begin with humans not God, nature not deity."[61]

8

THE CONFLICT
FROM HUMAN DESPAIR THROUGH
THE MOVE TOWARD GLOBALISM

The Results of the Denial

THE DENIAL OF GOD'S EXISTENCE OR relevancy that was caused by man's rejection of divine revelation has prompted radical changes of great consequence for society and the world.

Human Despair

First, it has caused despair for many people. This despair found expression in art, literature, music, philosophy, and some forms of theology beginning near the end of World War I and continuing through the end of the twentieth century. God created human beings with need of a personal relationship with Him for ultimate meaning and purpose in life. The denial of the personal God who controls history and moves it toward an ultimate good end has produced a spiritual void inside of people. It has led man to conclude that there is no ultimate good purpose for history or one's personal life. Science and materialism have not been able to provide humanity with a satisfying replacement for a personal God—a replacement that can give man ultimate meaning for life and comfort from fear of death.[1] As society seems to be falling apart in disorder and conflict, it appears to man that everything exists and happens purely by purposeless, unintelligent chance. Thus there is no rhyme or reason to this present existence.

In response to this despair, man tries desperately to find release or meaning through many vain means: alcohol, materialism, constant entertainment, fornication, adultery, homosexuality, lesbianism, drugs, witchcraft, spiritism, Satan worship, other forms of the occult, astrology, Oriental mysticism, transcendental meditation, yoga, some forms of music, New Age concepts, and false religions. Satan offers these and other things to fill the void and bring people under his influence. When individuals find that none of these things satisfies the need for ultimate meaning and purpose, in a sense of futility some turn to suicide. The denial of a personal God is leading man to preach the following message: "Vanity of vanities; all is vanity" (Eccl. 1:2).

Denial of Moral Absolutes

The denial of God's existence or relevancy has prompted the denial of moral absolutes that are binding upon all human beings. Man reasons that, if there is no personal God who has revealed moral absolutes to mankind, who holds persons responsible for their actions, and who will judge them in the future, then there can be no standards of morality to which people must conform. The traditional moral absolutes must have been developed by man in a past age that is no longer relevant to this one. Since man was the source of those absolutes, then man has the right to reject, change, or ignore them. Morality is a relative, not an absolute thing. It is relative to the attitude and circumstance of the individual. The *Humanifest Manifesto II* states, "We affirm that moral values derive their source from human experience. Ethics is autonomous and situational needing no theological or ideological sanction."[2]

Some influential persons claimed that the rejection of moral absolutes is beneficial. In the 1960s, God-is-dead theologian Thomas J. J. Altizer asserted that, in order for the world to move

into the new utopian age, mankind must reverse all the morality taught in the Bible. He called biblical morality "satanic."[3] In
the 1970s Professor Charles A. Reich of Yale University suggest-
ed that such things as use of drugs, sexual permissiveness,
pornography, and despising of productive work may help usher
in the new utopian age.[4]

As a result of this reasoning, society has experienced an incredible
breakdown of morality. Contrary to the absolutes God has revealed,
the idea that any sexual relationships outside the bonds of male-
female marriage are immoral is rejected, and advocates of that idea
are increasingly despised and threatened. There are movements to
legally redefine the historic concept of marriage and force society to
accept that redefinition, to abolish spanking of children and capital
punishment for murderers, to abolish or redefine the family, and to
protect the propagation of adult and child pornography. The killing
of unborn and partially born human beings has been legalized. Some
people insist that no moral issues are involved with assisted suicide,
human cloning, and the destruction of viable human embryos for the
sake of stem-cell research. Divorce, drunkenness, illegitimacy, and
free use of drugs have become widespread. Obscene language,
immodest dress, public display of nudity, stealing, lying, cheating,
and even sadomasochistic sex are increasingly condoned.
Permissiveness and lack of discipline have become the order of the
day. The foundation of society is threatened by this breakdown. A
computer scientist, who was a victim of violence, has asked "how
America could have deteriorated so quickly from a stable and order-
ly world into our current chaos of fatherlessness, illegitimacy,
divorce, violence, deviancy, and anything-goes morality."[5]

God created man (male and female) in His own image
(Gen. 1:26–28) and thereby gave man greater dignity than
any other earthly creature. As a result of rejecting divine revelation and God, man is losing that human dignity through
immorality. While praising this moral "freedom," man
becomes a slave to lusts.

The modern breakdown of morality is a repeat of what
Gentiles experienced in ancient times. In both instances the

breakdown was the result of willful rejection of divine revelation and the true and living God. Romans 1:18–32 indicates that, because Gentiles in ancient history willfully rejected divine revelation and God and developed false religions, God judged them by turning them over to uncleanness, shameful passions, and a reprobate mind, which resulted in the breakdown of morality, order, civility, and decency in society. This indicates that a society that experiences such breakdown is under a form of divine judgment because it willfully rejected God and His revelation.

Denial of Objective Truth

The denial of God's existence or relevancy has prompted the conclusion that there is no objective truth that is binding upon all mankind. The Scriptures declare that the God of the Bible is "the God of truth" (Ps. 31:5; Isa. 65:16) and that the revelation He has given to mankind is truth (the presentation of ultimate reality) (Ps. 119:160; Jn. 17:17; 2 Tim. 2:15). In light of this, the denial of God's existence prompts people to reason that there is no body of ultimate truth that exists apart from man and has been delivered to man by another source. Each individual determines what is truth for himself or herself. What is truth for one person is not truth for another. Thus truth is subjective and relative.

A 1969 book aimed at public school teachers states, "We now know that each man creates his own unique world, that he, and he alone, generates whatever reality he can ever know. . . . Among other things, this means that no man can ever be absolutely certain of anything. The best anyone can ever do is to say how something appears to *him*. The cosmos offers no absolute confirmations."[6] The "concept of absolute fixed, unchanging 'truth,' particularly from a polarizing good-bad perspective," is an "out-of-joint concept."[7]

Denial of an Objective Standard of Right and Wrong

This denial of objective truth has prompted the conclusion that there is no objective standard by which a person can evaluate whether something is right or wrong. Thus no person can legitimately tell another that what he or she has done is wrong. For example, a person should never tell another that his or her lifestyle is wrong, even though that lifestyle may cause premature death. And no one should ever tell teenagers that they should abstain from sex until marriage. No one has the right to impose his or her concept of right or wrong upon another.

This denial of objective truth and an objective standard of right and wrong is propagated through values clarification courses in grade schools, college and university courses, the media, Internet, publications, some forms of music, and the entertainment industry.

In the 1970s a former public school administrator showed me a sixth grade values clarification course text book. Immediately inside the front cover were three large symbols—the swastika of Naziism, the cross of Christianity, and the hammer and sickle of Communism. Underneath the symbols was the question, "Which of these is right?" The first half of the book communicated the following concept: no one can legitimately say that any of these is right or that any is wrong, because there is no objective standard by which a person can evaluate whether something is right or wrong. In the middle of the book was a quotation of the Ten Commandments from the Bible. The second half of the book indicated that people who believe in the Ten Commandments as a standard of right and wrong are out of touch with reality.

Shortly after the beginning of the twenty-first century, Scholastic, Inc., which publishes books for school children, began targeting Christian schools and parents with books related to faith. Some of the books are decent. But one, *Conversations With God for Teens,* presents questions that teenagers might address to God. The author gives what he imagines would be God's answers. For example: teen question—"Some of the kids are cheating in class, and on tests. They want me to join them. But I know that cheating is wrong." God's answer—"There is no such thing as 'right' and 'wrong,' as we discussed earlier. There is only what 'works' and what 'doesn't work,' given what you are trying to do."[8]

As a result of children being taught that there is no objective standard by which a person can evaluate whether something is right or wrong, students coming to college find it impossible to conclude that such things as human sacrifice and the Nazi killing of millions of people in the Holocaust are morally wrong. Tragically their moral relativism is intensified even more at many college and university campuses[9] that propagate the post-modern denial of any objective truth.

Growing Spirit of Anarchy or Lawlessness

There also is a growing spirit of anarchy or lawlessness in society. This is closely related to the denial of God, moral absolutes, objective truth, and an objective standard of right and wrong. Human beings are becoming progressively irritated with external restraints being placed upon their desires and conduct. They reason that, if there is no God ruling over man to control and judge human conduct, then other human beings and man-made institutions have no right to do that. Each individual should be free to do what is right in his or her own eyes when-ever and however he wants to.

Charles Darwin gave expression to this attitude when he said: "A man who has no assured and no present belief in the exis-tence of a personal God or a future existence with retribution and rewards, can have for his rule of life, as far as I can see, only to follow those impulses and instincts which are strongest or which seem to him the best ones."[10]

As a result of this attitude, human beings are acting more and more like spoiled, pampered children who throw violent temper tantrums if they cannot have what they want when they want it. Society is becoming characterized by road rage on highways; pas-senger rage on airplanes; killing of parents by children; violence in schools; killing of fellow workers and bosses by fired workers; drug related violence on streets, in neighborhoods, and homes. If there is no objective standard for determining right or wrong, then on what basis can a society or individual conclude that these kinds of violent acts are wrong and should be stopped?

New Concept of Tolerance

The denial of objective truth and an objective standard of right and wrong has prompted a movement to force society to accept a new concept of tolerance. The historic view of tolerance taught that people and groups of differing opinions and practices are to live together peaceably. They have the right to believe that a contrary opinion or practice is wrong and to openly express that belief, but they do not have the right to threaten, terrorize, or physically harm those with whom they disagree.

The new concept of tolerance asserts that the belief or open expression that an opinion or practice of a person or group is wrong amounts to a hate crime and should be punished by law. Powerful groups pressure state and national governments to make this new concept law by passing proposed antihate bills. Since laws against threatening, terrorizing, or physically harming people or groups of differing opinions and practices already exist, it is obvious that the goal of these proposed bills is to outlaw freedom of belief and speech. Passage of such bills have the potential of turning states and nations into police states comparable to those that adopted the Inquisition and Communism.

Police in one community in England enter "restaurants in disguise to listen for bigoted conversation. In the first week of 'Operation Napkin,' one man was arrested for unacceptable table talk. . . . Columnist John O'Sullivan, former editor of *National Review,* points out that George Orwell (in his book *1984*) foresaw a nation in which the most serious crimes would not be rape or robbery but 'thought crimes.' O'Sullivan wrote: 'And the evidence for thought-crimes has to be sought in the nearest equivalent to thoughts: private conversations.' Last year, he noted, an official British report proposed criminalizing racist remarks made in the family home."[11]

The Boy Scouts of America paid a high price because of this new view of tolerance. When an assistant scoutmaster publicly revealed that he was homosexual, the Scouts asked for his resignation. Homosexuality violated the Scout Oath to be "morally straight" and the values that the Scouts wished to develop in boys. As a result of this stand, the United Way and many other longtime supporting organizations withdrew financial support. The Scouts were evicted from public facility meeting places and denounced widely by the media. They were forced to defend their stand in court. The New Jersey Supreme Court unanimously ruled against them, but the United States Supreme Court, with a 5-4 vote, ruled in their favor. The majority justices indicated that this was an issue of freedom of speech.[12]

This new view of tolerance has prompted businesses, education, and other institutions to require all employees, faculty, and students to attend minority, gender, and gay sensitivity training sessions. It has impacted what elementary school children are taught in public schools. Some versions of elementary school sex-education courses are designed to persuade children to regard homosexuality and lesbianism as legitimate lifestyles. Some of the courses contain detailed sexual instruction provided by The Gay Men's Health Crisis organization. Concerning this, authoress and editor, Midge Decter, stated, "This effort to teach so-called tolerance for those whose 'lifestyle' might be different from the one known to the child within his own family has resulted in a number of pedagogic crimes against the young."[13]

Women's Liberation Movement

There is an attempt to annul distinctive roles and appearances that God ordained for the sexes. This has prompted the development of the Women's Liberation Movement.

Secular feminists have concluded that, since there is no God who created man as male and female and revealed distinctive roles and appearances for the sexes, then the traditional distinctions that have been followed for centuries were man-made, devised in past times by the male for the purpose of keeping the female in subjection. Since man was their source, man may reject or change those distinctions.

The secular phase of the movement has produced major changes in the workplace. Women have been able to gain leadership positions in businesses that formerly were held exclusively by men. In the realm of government women have been appointed or elected to key positions in executive, legislative, and judicial branches. In the field of education some have become chairpersons of departments, board members, and even presidents of colleges and universities.

Authoress and editor Midge Decter has stated, "Even at its mildest, however, the women's movement demands that women be given the right to seek freedom by redefining sex, marriage, motherhood, and career in whatever way they find least psychologically and physically burdensome to themselves."[14]

In addition, Decter declared, "Ideally the movement would impose regulations without end on all the relations between men and women, and boys and girls, in everyday life" and "has managed . . . to impose regulations aplenty."[15] Some examples: the United States Supreme Court has required the Jaycees and Rotary Clubs to open their memberships to women.[16]

Feminist educators at some universities have developed a plan that would overhaul every campus department and curriculum to be "woman-friendly," require every academic department to "hold an annual seminar on gender issues," require all faculty and students to "undergo gender sensitivity training," require all teaching styles to be "woman-friendly," forbid curriculum from being "overrepresented" by men, modify traditional academic freedom, and punish noncomplying teachers with denial of "promotions, raises and other benefits."[17]

In the military realm the United States Army tried mixed-gender training for five years but abandoned it as a failure in 1982. But feminist political pressure caused it to be reinstalled in 1994. As a result, basic training was reconfigured so that "anybody can get through," largely in "response to women's high rates of injury and inability to meet the old standards."[18] The Pentagon lowered standards, instituted some double standards, and redefined basic training "success" in terms of what women did well. A new concept of "comparable effort" enables a female trainee, who does not perform as well as a male in a physical task, to receive equal or higher scores than the male.[19]

John Leo stated, "Fake scores and the degradation of basic training are a disaster for the military. Mixed-gender training has nothing to do with combat readiness. It has to do with politics and the desire to show absolute equality even where it doesn't exist and can't."[20]

In the realm of relationships, male bashing has become a society phenomenon. Christina Hoff-Sommers, authoress of *Who Stole Feminism*, points out that a double standard has developed in male-female conflict. She stated, "There used to be a certain level of good-natured teasing between the sexes. Now, even the most innocent remark about women will get you in trouble but there's no limit at all to what you can say about men."[21]

Humorous and nonhumorous hostile comments about men keep growing with very little objections. Media hints that a woman who has been jilted might want to consider violent action against the man escape protest. Antimale greetings cards become increasingly hostile toward men, including a humorous one of women suffocating men to death.[22] Cathy Young, *Detroit News* columnist, noted a swelling expanse of male bashing in calendars and women's magazines.[23]

Anthropologist Lionel Tiger claims that "the long campaign of public denunciation of men by activist women is not encouraging men to take more responsibility. The fact is that it's not that easy being a guy these days."[24] In addition, Tiger asserts that the birth control pill gave women sexual freedom from having to be bound to one male in marriage throughout life and "placed into question existing moral and religious systems that focused on controlling sexual behavior."[25] And good paying careers have made it possible for women to be free from dependence upon a husband to be a provider.

The combination of all these things has given men "less and less control of the impact of their own sexuality" and caused them to question the purpose of their role as a man in society.[26] As a result, more men are "abandoning their role of being good providers" and "real fathers" for children, and there is "a higher divorce rate."[27] Tiger asserts that this trend may have devastating long-term results for children. "Daughters must now be raised to take care of themselves," and it is especially devastating "for raising boys."[28] He points out that David Popenoe emphasizes this in his book, *Life Without Father*, which is "a plea for restoring traditional forms of fatherhood."[29]

Researchers and other authorities are beginning to emphasize that boys are the people most at risk from the effects of the Women's Liberation Movement. John Leo claims that "the worst impact of all the male bashing is on the young."[30] He relates the experiences of Barbara Wilder-Smith, a teacher and researcher in the Boston area. She made "Boys Are Good" T-shirts for boys in her class, but all ten of her female student teachers objected to the message. She claimed that people who would see her son wear the T-shirt would "object strongly and shout things," but there was no objection to derogatory messages by girls against boys. The worst thing is the fact that many adolescent boys would not wear the T-shirts because the male-bashing cultural messages have convinced them that "something is seriously wrong with being a male."[31]

Feminist leader Gloria Steinem said, "We need to raise boys like we raise girls."[32] That kind of feminist thinking has prompted efforts to feminize boys. Schools are one place where such efforts have been put into practice. In her book *The War Against Boys: How Misguided Feminism Is Harming Our Young Men*, Christina Hoff-Sommers demonstrates that studies that claim that girls are at greatest risk in schools have it in reverse. Through specific data she shows that it is boys who are at greatest risk in schools.[33]

Feminist-minded educators have constructed school philosophies of education, curricula, and activities contrary to the abounding energy and competitive nature of boys. Marvin Olasky points out that an "anti-competition bias" that impacts children exists in schools. He states, "At many schools the classic competitions are dead. Dodge ball is out. Despite the high profile of the National Spelling Bee, classroom spelling bees are much less frequent. At some elementary-school basketball games no one keeps score."[34] His point is that this approach is contrary to the way that boys are naturally geared to learn. Thus he states, "What New Age facilitators don't realize is that friendship grows fastest when boys are working side by side with the common goal of winning, not sitting in a circle sharing their feelings. Competition also builds leadership."[35] And "what's mainly needed is an attitude adjustment among educators. They need to understand that since boys have enormous energy, teachers should channel the current, not fight it. . . . We need to raise boys to be boys."[36]

Some religious feminists claim that Jesus' male successors overthrew His teaching by creating "a males-only power structure in the church."[37] This view is causing radical changes in the realm of theology.

By 1989 eighty-four Christian denominations had ordained women as pastors.[38] In 1989 the first female bishop was appointed in the worldwide Anglican Communion.[39] Some feminists have questioned if a woman can be saved by a male Savior and have adopted a new crucifix with a nude woman named Christa nailed to the cross.[40] Some reject the generic noun "mankind" and substitute "Creator, Redeemer, and Comforter" or "Mother, Lover, and Friend" in place of the designations "Father, Son, and Holy Spirit."[41] According to one observer, "The prime goal of Christian feminists . . . is a thorough and comprehensive transformation of the language, symbols and sacred texts of the Christian faith—and therefore of the faith itself."[42] They have influenced some translators and Bible publishers to produce genderless language Bibles.

In November 1993 approximately 2,100 women, including female theologians, two dozen Presbyterian Church (U.S.A.) national staff members, and 56 top United Methodist officials, attended a "Re-Imagining" conference that "denounced the Christian church and its teachings as the source of racism, sexism, classism, heterosexism, human violence and environmental destruction."[43] The conference was characterized by negative comments about the names "Jesus, the Father, Son and Holy Spirit"; ridicule of blood atonement; an expression of pantheism; celebration of lesbianism; a call to reinvent the family; and replacement of communion with a service of milk and honey devoted to "Our maker, Sophia." The leader sang, "Our mother, Sophia, we are women in your image." The crowd responded, "Sophia Creator God, Let your milk and honey flow, Sophia, Creator God, Shower us with your love."[44]

Feminist biblical scholar Elizabeth Achtemeier criticized such "mother metaphors for God because they resurrect the Near Eastern fertility goddesses whom the authors of the Hebrew Bible rejected in proclaiming a Creator who is qualitatively different from his creation."[45]

Push for Unity

The denial of God's existence and divine revelation of truth has prompted the growing conviction that the goal of mankind should be unity. During the twentieth century two world wars involved the armed forces of many nations and brought unparalleled massive destruction and loss of life to large areas of the world. Genocide was practiced on a grand scale against various ethnic groups. Multinational forces intervened militarily in the Far East (Korean and Vietnam Wars), Middle East (The Gulf War), and Europe (Bosnia and Kosovo). Warfare technology developed nuclear weapons and delivery systems. With such doomsday weapons possessed by two opposing superpowers, the Cold War continuously had the potential of destroying all life on earth throughout most of the second half of the twentieth century. The twenty-first century has continued the tragic saga of man's inhumanity to man. A new kind of warfare, Islamic-related terrorism driven by the commitment to cause all of humanity to submit to Islamic rule, threatens the world.

Because there seems to be no end to continuous conflicts that threaten the existence of humanity, many conclude that, since there is no God who can intervene and bring lasting peace to the world, then man must solve the problem. *The Humanist Manifesto II* states, "No deity will save us; we must save ourselves."[46] They also conclude that the only way that man can save himself from suffering and destruction is to unite all of humanity into a common, human community.[47] There must be a movement toward one-world government and a single church or religion.[48] All differences of opinion and convictions that divide man must be abolished.[49]

In line with this thinking, *The Humanist Manifesto II* states, "We deplore the division of humankind on nationalistic grounds. We have reached a turning point in history where the best option is to transcend the limits of national sovereignty and to move toward the building of a world community in which all sectors of the human family can participate. Thus we look to the development of a system of world law and a world order based upon transnational federal government."[50] Finally it states, "Commitment to all humankind is the highest commitment of which we are capable; it transcends the narrow allegiances of church, state, party, class, or race in moving toward a wider vision of human potentiality. What more daring a goal for humankind than for each person to become, in ideal as well as practice, a citizen of a world community."[51]

Prospect of Unified World Community

In light of these statements, it is interesting to note that the world is moving rapidly toward the formation of a global village. International institutions, such as the World Court, were established to judge actions and disputes of nations and leaders, and the United Nations was formed to provide a forum whereby nations could solve differences without war. Other factors that make the formation of a unified world community appear possible are long-range airplanes that make travel to most areas of the world possible within one day; telephones, satellites, computers, fax machines, and e-mail that make instant, worldwide communication possible between people, governments, and businesses; television and radio that bring the sight and sound of world events into homes; the European Union, which is forging a form of unification with a common economic system, currency, and the possibility of eventual political and military union; and the advancing internationalization of economics. The threat of worldwide terrorism may drive civilization toward a unified world government for the sake of survival.

The increasing globalization of the world imposes a growing concern for what happens worldwide. In light of this concern, on September 6–8, 2000, approximately 150 world leaders gathered at the United Nations world headquarters for the United Nations Millennium Summit. This was the largest gathering of world leaders in the history of mankind.[52] The stated purpose of this summit was to make globalization "fully inclusive and equitable" by getting world leaders and their nations to commit to the goals of freeing all peoples of the world from want and fear, protecting the environment from destruction, and renewing the United Nations.[53] The summit ended with world leaders unanimously adopting the *United Nations Millennium Declaration,* which "contains a statement of values, principles and objectives for the international agenda for the twenty-first century."[54]

Satan will try to establish a visible, political form of his kingdom rule over the entire world with all mankind united under a one-world government and dominant ruler, the Antichrist. He will attempt to establish this during the last seven years prior to the Second Coming of Christ. The world is moving rapidly toward the formation of a global village. In addition, the growing convictions that the goal of mankind should be unit; that the only way man can save himself from suffering and destruction is to unite all of humanity into a common, human community; and that there must be a movement toward one-world government all indicate that the world is moving in the direction that Satan wants. The groundwork is being prepared for him to attempt to obtain his goal.

Religious Pluralism—Move Toward One-World Religion

The denial of the existence of God and divine revelation has prompted a widespread spirit of religious pluralism. Increasing numbers of people are claiming that in the realm of religion there can be no theological absolutes. Since there is no personal God, there never has been a divine revelation of theological truth or of any religion. All dogmas and religions are man-made; therefore, they are relative. The idea that a particular faith is the only true one because it alone was divinely revealed must be rejected. Exclusive claims of only one true

God, one true religion, and one way are a divisive form of intolerant bigotry. Since all religions are man-made, all must be respected and regarded as equal. Attempts to convert people from one religion to another should be stopped.

Some people declare that, in order to totally unify mankind and prevent future wars motivated by religion, there should be a single world church or religion.[55] The threat of Islamic-related terrorism to the world may prompt many more people to advocate this.

The twentieth century witnessed significant developments of an ecumenical nature in the religious realm. These included interdenominational cooperation; unions of denominations; national federations of church groups, such as the National Council of Churches; international councils and fellowships, such as the World Council of Churches; dialogues between groups within organized Christendom; dialogues between Christendom and non-Christian religions; Catholic observers at World Council of Churches' meetings; Protestant observers at Roman Catholic meetings; and joint participation of Protestants, Catholics, and people of other religions in large public rallies.

In October 1999 representatives of 20 religions from 48 nations met at the Vatican to explore cooperative opportunities in the new millennium. Non-Christian attendees included Jews, Muslims, Hindus, Buddhists, Sikhs, Zoroastrians, Mandaeans, Jains, Shintoists, Confucians, Bahai's, representatives of traditional religions, and several Japanese faiths. Organized Christendom attendees came from the following groups: Roman Catholic; Anglican; Lutheran; Reformed; Mennonite; evangelical; and Greek, Armenian, Romanian, and Assyrian Orthodox.[56]

Anglican and Roman Catholic bishops from thirteen world regions met in May 2000 to form "a joint commission to consider unification."[57]

The Episcopal Church and the Evangelical Lutheran Church (America's largest Lutheran denomination) approved an alliance "to share clergy and sacraments, and work together in 'shared mission.'"[58]

Roman Catholic and Eastern Orthodox leaders from around the world met in July 2000 "to seek common ground" with the prospect of "eventual complete reconciliation."[59]

Three hundred representatives of 39 religions met in June 2000 under the leadership of Episcopal Bishop William Swing to sign a charter establishing the United Religions Initiative. The URI asserts that all religions derive their wisdom from the same source.[60] This implies that all religions have a common base for unification. In 1995 Bishop Swing declared that, as the world is progressing toward "unity in terms of global economy, global media and global ecological system," one thing is missing—"a global soul."[61] In other words, a unified world will need a unified religion.

One thousand representatives of religions from around the world met August 28–31, 2000, at the United Nations for the Millennium World Peace Summit of Religious and Spiritual Leaders. The purpose of this summit was to create "an international Advisory Council of Religious and Spiritual Leaders that is designed to serve as an ongoing interfaith ally to the U.N. in its quest for peace, global understanding and international cooperation."[62]

The secretary-general of this religious summit, Bawa Jain, worked with United Nations Secretary-General Kofi Annan and his office to arrange this gathering. Jain is a leader in Bishop Swing's United Religions Initiative.[63] Jain expressed belief that all religions are equal, that claims of absolute truth must be dealt with, and that all attempts to convert people from one religion to another should be outlawed. He stated that the timing of the religious summit one week before the United Nations' Millennium Summit of world political leaders was perfect, because it afforded religious leaders the opportunity to show political leaders "how to usher in the peace of the new world order through religious universalism."[64]

This religious summit received heavy support from Ted Turner, founder of CNN, and Canadian billionaire Maurice Strong. In his speech at the summit Turner told how he rejected the Christian faith he was taught as a child because of its intolerant claim to be the only true religion.[65] Strong, who is senior advisor both to the secretary-general of the United Nations and the president of the World Bank, is so influential in global affairs that *New Yorker Magazine* stated, "The survival of civilization in something like its present form might depend significantly on the efforts of a single man."[66]

Representatives of several religions reacted negatively to the summit's emphasis that all religions are equal and that there should be no attempts to convert people from one religion to another. Less than two weeks after the summit the Vatican's Congregation for the Doctrine of the Faith issued a 36-page document that declared that the Roman Catholic Church is the only "instrument of the salvation of all humanity," that non-Christian religions are "gravely deficient" as a means of salvation, and that most non-Catholic Christian denominations are not "churches in the proper sense."[67]

In September 2000 more than 160 Jewish leaders from all major branches of Judaism signed "a landmark statement acknowledging Judaism's shared roots with Christianity and calling on Jews to give up distrust of Christians."[68]

Two thousand representatives of "Orthodox, Roman Catholic, Anglican, Reformation Protestant, Pentecostal, and evangelical churches as well as Christian networks and para-church organizations" from around the world met September 9–11, 2000, to explore the possibility of forming a "global Christian forum" that would address issues of common concern and "foster relationships that could lead to common ministry."[69]

In September 2000 leaders of the National Council of Churches, the National Association of Evangelicals, and possibly the Roman Catholic ecumenical affairs office in Washington were considering meeting in the future to study the possibility of forming "a new broad-based national ecumenical body that would work together on common social causes."[70]

The secular and religious developments toward the unity of mankind and globalization take on more significance when viewed from a biblical perspective. Revelation 17—18 reveals that a global political-economic-religious system will dominate the world during the future Tribulation Period. The political division (the beast) will tolerate domination by the

religious division (the harlot, which has global influence—
17:15) as long as it needs the influence of that division to help
it attain complete global domination (17:3, 7). But once that
goal is reached the political division will turn against and
destroy the religious division (17:16).

According to Vatican expert Malachi Martin, powerful cardinals
in the Vatican have formed an alliance with "leaders of major international humanist organizations," such as "academia, foundations,
nongovernment organizations, even some governmental agencies."
These cardinals and humanist leaders have a "globalist view." They
believe that the Roman Catholic Church is "the only global structure" that is able "to act as a stabilizing social force in the world."
Thus the humanist leaders hope that "they can get the Roman
Catholic Church to side with them" in fulfilling their globalist
view.[71] If this be true, then one can expect that globalism will
increasingly pressure religious groups to unite with the Roman
Catholic Church to form a one-world church.

Religious pluralism lays the foundation for people to reason
as follows: Since all religions are man-made, not divinely
revealed, then there would be nothing wrong with man merging
all religions together to form a one-world religion for the sake of
unifying all mankind. That would be the wise thing to do to
bring peace and harmony to the world. By laying that foundation religious pluralism conditions people to accept not only the
harlot religious system (Rev. 17), but also the one-world religion
of Antichrist worship (Dan. 11:36–37; 2 Th. 2:3–4; Rev. 13:5–8)
that will destroy and replace the harlot religious system.

Persecution of Christians
The denial of the existence of the God of the Bible and biblical revelation has prompted increasing hostility toward and severe persecution of Christians at many places around the world. This war of
Christians is being carried out by Communist governments in
China, North Korea, and Vietnam; by Hindus in India; and Muslims
in numerous nations in Asia, the Middle East, and Africa. Orthodox
religious leaders instigate persecution against evangelical Christians

in Eastern European nations, and Roman Catholic leaders do the same in some Central and South American nations.

In some instances Christians are forbidden to gather together for group worship, distribute Christian literature and Bibles, and witness to non-Christians. In many places they are arrested, imprisoned, threatened, tortured, mutilated, and killed. Others are forced to flee from their homes and sources of income. Christian women and children are kidnapped and sold into slavery. Many Christian women and girls are raped because of their faith. Churches and homes are destroyed. Christian hospitals and schools are bombed.

In Western European nations and North America there is a growing hostility particularly toward evangelical Christians who hold to historic, biblical Christianity and, in some instances, toward Roman Catholics. Many schools, colleges, and universities allow views, practices, and lifestyles that are contrary to and even anti-Christian. These views and practices are allowed to be represented, expressed, and even advocated by faculty, students, and outsiders. But representations, expressions, and advocacy of Christianity are forbidden. Bibles, clothing, and other articles that may carry some expression of Christian faith are taboo in many public schools. Christian children are often forbidden to give any reference to their faith in oral or written projects.

In the workplace workers are often required to attend sensitivity training sessions, some of which advocate acceptance of lifestyles that violate biblical morality. If they object to such sessions, they are subjected to rebuke, ridicule, and in some instances forms of discipline or threat of loss of employment. Some Christian nurses are fired for refusing to participate in abortion procedures. Some men have been fired from longstanding positions once their biblical view on homosexuality became known.

A qualified, black football coach who sought the head coaching position at a large secular university was rejected early in the interview process because his Christian views were not compatible with the university's liberal student body and active gay community. The coach was surprised at how bluntly the university expressed its reason for not considering him. He said officials wouldn't have told him if they were discriminating against him because he is black. But they had no hesitation about telling him it was because of his Christian beliefs.[72] A student writer pointed out the irony of a liberal university that stands for inclusion and diversity using Christian beliefs as a reason for rejecting a prospective coach.[73]

Because evangelical Christians claim that biblical Christianity is the only true religion; take a stand against the great moral decline in society; and oppose the radical agenda that liberal, secular extremists are trying to force upon it, they increasingly are subject to vicious attacks. In May 2002 Joel Belz called attention to "the growing disdain many sophisticates in American culture hold for evangelical Christians. The big media in our society, along with higher academia, have habitually over the last six months compared conservative Christians to the radical Taliban. 'When you've seen one fundamentalist,' these folks tend to say, 'you've seen them all.'"[74]

Gene Edward Veith pointed out the contradictory nature of the comparison of conservative Christians with the terrorist Taliban. He wrote that in that comparison, "those whose theology motivates them to try to save innocent lives are portrayed as being the same as those whose theology motivates them to kill innocent lives. Those who call for good music are lumped with those who want to abolish music altogether. A religion that has brought freedom wherever it goes is branded as the same as a religion that has brought tyranny. Christians exercising their constitutional liberty to express their convictions in the public square are identified as terrorists."[75]

Veith indicated that this attack on Christians should be identified as "religious bigotry," "religious intolerance," "secularist extremism," and "theological terrorism." But he also warned that, if this attack succeeds in convincing the public that the war on terrorism is a war against religion itself, "it lays the groundwork for actual religious persecution."[76]

Denial of Christ's Deity

The denial of God's existence and divine revelation has also prompted a tendency to completely humanize Jesus Christ. People have concluded that, since there is no sovereign, personal God or divine revelation, then Jesus Christ was neither a divine being incarnated in human flesh nor an incredible revelation of God to man.

In light of this conclusion, the counter-culture movement of the 1960s and '70s portrayed Jesus as the Great Revolutionary who wore long hair and a beard, trained a band of revolutionaries, and refused to take employment so that He could be free to roam the countryside fighting the establishment of His day. He was pictured on posters as a fugitive, wanted by the government for His subversive activities. His death was regarded as an example of what the establishment does to those who oppose it. Thus the counter-culture movement portrayed Jesus as its Superstar in order to inspire people to fight against what it regarded as the establishment of that time.

Modern stage and motion picture productions have portrayed Jesus as a man who deceived himself into thinking that he was a divine messiah, but who had the same faults, lusts and passions as other men.

The New Age Movement teaches that Jesus was a man, not the "Christ Spirit." He was not different from other human beings. He was not a divine Savior who died for the sins of mankind. He was divine in the same sense that all human beings are divine. He did not experience physical resurrection.[77]

Deification of Man

The denial of the personal God of the Bible has prompted the development of a pantheistic, religious attitude that deifies man. Man has the inherent need to worship something. Since he has rejected the personal God, the only thing left for him to worship is the material world of which he is the highest, supposedly-evolved representative. Thus man is concluding that the secular realm is the sacred one.[78] Since man is the highest form of life that exists, then man should be regarded and worshiped as God.

The trend toward a pantheism that deifies man can be seen in the statements of several modern thinkers. Protestant God-is-dead theologian Thomas J. J. Altizer stated that, since man has denied the existence of a personal God, he must as a race achieve human self-transcendence, which is "man-godhood."[79] Thus, according to Altizer, the world cannot move into the new utopian age until we as human beings do three things— acknowledge that the God of the Bible is dead, reverse all the morality taught in the Bible, and "acclaim ourselves as 'the Great Humanity Divine.'"[80]

John Cooper wrote that theology must see the transcendent within this world; it must be based on a philosophy that recognizes no other world.[81]

Roman Catholic scholar Pierre Teilhard de Chardin stated that humanity is evolving into a collectivity of fellowship that will end ultimately in the unity of God and man.[82] He concluded that, when a person loves the earth and especially loves man who is the crown of the evolution of the earth, he is loving God.[83] Teilhard believed that scientific studies, communications, the growth of liberal social democracy, and the increasing dependence of man upon man that draws them into socialistically based communities, are forces that contribute to the growth of corporate humanity. In this corporate humanity "all men are to become part of one living organism that covers the face of the world."[84] Thus the God to be worshiped is the one who will arise out of the eternally evolving human race.[85] In other words, according to Teilhard, man is becoming God through the evolutionary process.

Liberal theology taught that man has a spark of divinity within him.

The New Age movement teaches that all human beings are "innately divine."[86]

In the middle of the future Tribulation Period, Satan's ultimate man, the Antichrist, will blaspheme the God of the Bible, claim that he is God, and demand that everyone worship him as God (Dan. 7:8, 19–20, 24–25; 9:27; 11:36—37; 2 Th. 2:3–4; Rev. 13:4–8). Through the development of an attitude that deifies man Satan is beginning to condition the minds of people to accept the future claim of Antichrist to be God and to worship him.

Denial of Man's Sin Nature

Denial of the existence of the God of the Bible and divine revelation has prompted the denial of the sinful nature of man. Man has concluded that, since there is no sovereign, personal God, there never was an original sin of rebellion against Him. The biblical story of the fall of man is a myth; therefore, there was not a time in history when man received a corrupt nature. Instead of possessing a sinful nature, man is essentially good. He has some of the instincts of the lower forms of life from which he has evolved. But as the process of evolution continues, man overcomes more and more of these animal instincts. Thus one can expect improvement in man's actions.

This has been the thinking of liberal theology. Similarly, the New Age movement teaches that in essence sin and evil do not exist. So man does not need a personal savior who died to redeem him from sin and its penalty. The ultimate cause of human predicaments is people forgetting their divinity. And the essence of salvation "is the realization of one's own divinity."[87]

This denial of man's sinful nature has led many to the false conclusion that humanity can live together as one harmonious unit without war, bigotry, and injustice if properly educated and if there is a radical change in the social order. That new order must consist of the complete unification of mankind under a one-world government and a one-world religion. On the basis of this same denial, many naive souls have assumed that, if one nation lays down its arms and refuses to fight, all other nations will do the same.

History demonstrates several things concerning the sinful nature of man. First, that nature is reality; it actually exists. Second, that nature, not the social order, is the root cause of man's inhumanity to man. Third, that sinful nature cannot be eradicated by education or a social order.

All human beings, including government and religious leaders, have that sinful nature. Powerful positions of authority can have a corrupting influence upon leaders. Such influence has prompted some leaders to allow their sinful natures to turn them into dictatorial tyrants who will wage war and kill millions of people in order to enforce their wills upon others. History demonstrates that, if one nation threatened by such a tyrant lays down its arms and refuses to fight, the tyrant will easily bring that nation under his dictatorial rule. He will not lay down his arms and stop fighting. It also demonstrates that the only way a tyrant can be stopped from enforcing his dictatorial rule over others is through a powerful force that can overthrow him. If, for example, there had not been such a force in the 1940s to overthrow Hitler, his atrocities would have wreaked genocide and other havoc over greater masses of humanity for many more years. For the sake of mankind the world needs a balance of power to stop and overthrow dictatorial tyrants.

If the powerful position of authority over one nation can corrupt its leader into becoming a dictatorial tyrant, then surely the powerful position of authority over a one-world government could corrupt its leader into becoming an unprecedented dictatorial tyrant with unparalleled, unlimited powers. With a one-world government, the entire world would be subject to his rule. There would be no balance of power in the world, no powerful opposing force that could overthrow him or stop any tyrannical, cruel policies or atrocities that he would choose to inflict. A one-world government would be an irresistible opportunity for that kind of person to come to power. The Bible indicates that, as the world moves in the direction of a unified, one-world government, that is the kind of ruler who will come to power.

Man's denial of the personal God of the Bible is proving to be no small matter. It is producing earthshaking, revolutionary results. The tragedy is that man believes he is following great wisdom in making this denial (Rom. 1:18–25; 1 Cor. 1:21). The truth is that he is being blinded by Satan, the god of this age (2 Cor. 4:4). Satan is using the results of man's denial to prepare the world for his coming attempt to establish the visible, political form of his kingdom on earth.

Thus, although the media calls the present conflict of issues in society "a cultural war," in reality it is a spiritual war that centers on two opposing world-life views. One of those views has the existence of the personal, sovereign, creator God of the Bible and divine revelation as its starting point and foundation. The other view has the denial of the existence of the God of the Bible and divine revelation as its starting point and foundation.

While Satan continues his work, God also is busy saving individuals from Satan's kingdom and adding them to the true Church—that body of people who personally have believed the gospel of Jesus Christ revealed in the Bible by placing their trust in Him alone for salvation from sin and eternal judgment.

What should Christians be doing in light of these revolutionary results of the denial of God in society? Christ has given one commission to the Church, and He has not changed it. We should be making every effort to evangelize the world with the gospel of Jesus Christ defined in 1 Corinthians 15:1–8 (Mk. 16:15), to ground believers in the rest of God's truth by systematically teaching them God's Word (Mt. 28:19–20; Eph. 4:11–12), and to pray earnestly for God to send a great spiritual awakening that will be instigated, governed, and empowered by the Holy Spirit and completely conformed to God's thoughts, ways, and truth.

The Conflict From the Rapture of the Church to Eternity Future

The Rapture of the True Church

WHEN THE TIME COMES FOR GOD to prepare Israel for restoration to her original place of blessing, His purpose for the true Church in the world will have been fulfilled. Thus, at an unannounced time, Jesus Christ will return to the air above the earth and, in an instantaneous moment, will resurrect from the dead all true Christians who have died, transform the bodies of all true Christians still living, and snatch both groups out of the world together. The Christians will meet Jesus in the air and return with Him to heaven (Jn. 14:1–3; 1 Cor. 15:51–52; 1 Th. 4:13–17). This great event has been called the Rapture of the Church. According to the Scriptures, it is the next prophetic event to be fulfilled.

Although the true Church is part of organized Christendom, it by no means comprises all of Christendom. Satan has sown many false professors of Christianity among the true believers. Thus, when the true Church is raptured out of the world, a large segment of Christendom will be left. Its entire membership will be comprised of people from Satan's kingdom. With the true believers gone, these false professors will have no difficulty in uniting all of Christendom into one, great, apostate religion with its headquarters located in one great city (Rev. 17).

The Seventieth Week of Daniel

After the rapture of the Church, the world will enter a unique seven-year period, the latter half of which will be characterized by great, unprecedented tribulation (Mt. 24:21). Because Daniel foretold that this period would be the last of seventy periods of seven years planned by God for Israel, it has been called the seventieth week of Daniel. Because it will be characterized by tribulation, others have called it the Tribulation Period.

Satan's Purposes for the Seventieth Week

In his war against the kingdom of God, Satan will have four major purposes for the seventieth week.

The Permanent Establishment of a Visible, Political Form of His Kingdom. Satan's first purpose will be to establish permanently and worldwide a visible, political form of his kingdom. In order to do this, he must have a king who will rule this kingdom for him. This king must be a man who will do what Christ refused to do—turn himself over to Satan's control in order to rule the kingdoms of the world (Mt. 4:8–10).

Satan will have such a man, but it will not be possible for that man to be revealed until two things happen (2 Th. 2:3, 6–7). First, there must be the "falling away" (literally, "the apostasy" (2 Th. 2:3). Before the world will be ready to accept Satan's man as its ruler, man must experience "the falling away" from God. In past time there have been limited apostasies or fallings away from God, but the fact that this future falling away has the definite article "the" indicates that it will be the ultimate apostasy. It will be ultimate in the sense that it will be a total, worldwide falling away from God in contrast with past limited apostasies. When the Rapture of the Church takes place, every saved person will be removed from the earth. As a result, instantly the entire world will be apostate because the earth will be filled exclusively with unsaved people. Thus the "falling away" will be the result of the Rapture of the Church.

Second, before Satan's man can be revealed, the Restrainer must be taken out of the way (2 Th. 2:6–7). Although Satan has worked desperately throughout history, he never has been able to accomplish his desires fully. The Holy Spirit has restrained the activities of his kingdom continually.[1] At the time that the Church is raptured and the world is left to the members of Satan's kingdom only, the Holy Spirit will cease His restraining work. As a result, Satan's man will be revealed to the world.

This man is given several names in the Bible, and each name reveals an aspect of his character. He is called the Antichrist by the apostle John. As the Antichrist, he will propagate man's present lie by denying the existence of the personal God and denying that Jesus Christ was God incarnate in human flesh (1 Jn. 2:18, 22; 4:3; 2 Jn. 7).

Daniel called this man the willful king (Dan. 11:36), and Paul named him the lawless one (2 Th. 2:3, 8). These titles indicate that he will be the ultimate expression of the current spirit of anarchy and lawlessness. He will tolerate no external restraints upon his own desires and no law except his own. He will demand that everyone do what he wants when he wants it. Like a spoiled child who throws a tantrum, he will vent his wrath upon everyone who dares to oppose him.

Paul also called him the son of perdition (2 Th. 2:3). As a son receives his nature from his parents, so this one will receive his nature from Satan, his spiritual father, the source of all evil that deserves perdition. He will be energized and controlled by Satan in such a way that he will perform the will of that great revolutionary (2 Th. 2:9; Rev. 13:4). Having denied the existence of God, he will turn himself over to Satan to find meaning and purpose for life. Satan will empower him to be his superstar.

Antichrist will have an amazing career. He will become the head of a revived form of the Roman Empire. Initially this empire will consist of a federation of ten divisions (Dan. 2:40–43; 7:23–25; Rev. 13:1; 17:12–13). Through an impressive display of the supernatural powers given to him by Satan, he will deceive the Western world into believing the lie that he is the answer to all of its problems (2 Th. 2:8–12). No doubt he will promise to unite humanity, bring law and order, radically change the social order, abolish injustice and poverty, bring total peace through the union of nations under one government, and solve the problems of pollution and population explosion in exchange for all authority being turned over to him. Being convinced that he has the powers necessary to fulfill his promises, and being frantic over its own failures to cope with the problems that seem to threaten mankind, the Western world will acclaim Antichrist to be its savior-messiah and will grant absolute control to him. No doubt any who object to this dictatorship will be called an enemy of mankind.

In his rise to power, Antichrist will ally himself with the one apostate religion of the western world for the purpose of gaining the powerful support of it and its people (Rev. 17). In addition, in the beginning of his rule as head of the Western world, Antichrist will make a seven-year covenant with the nation of Israel, guaranteeing her protection from her enemies and freedom to reestablish her Old Testament worship (Dan. 9:27). Because of this promised protection, Israel will phase out her defense program and focus her attention upon peaceful pursuits (Ezek. 37:11, 14). She will rebuild the Temple in Jerusalem and reinstitute her Old Testament sacrifices. Thus, during the first three and one-half years of his reign, Antichrist will appear to be very benevolent to most people in the Western world, the apostate church, and Israel.

Satan will inspire Antichrist to pursue the goal of a worldwide kingdom. However, in his attempt to reach this goal, Antichrist will be opposed by a huge military power north of Israel. Sometime before the middle of the seventieth week Syria and Egypt will challenge Antichrist's guarantee of protection to Israel by invading that land from the north and the south (Dan. 11:40). It may be that these nations will be persuaded to do this by the power to the north. In reaction to this invasion, Antichrist will rush his Western army to the Middle East, crush Syria, and march south to invade Egypt (Dan. 11:40–43). While conquering Egypt, he will hear disturbing news out of the east and the north (Dan. 11:44).

The disturbing news may be to the effect that the great power north of Israel, together with allied forces, has invaded Israel in response to the Western world's intrusion into the Middle East (Ezek. 38:1–16). When Antichrist will receive this news in Egypt, he will rush his armies north toward Israel with the goal of furiously destroying the northern invader and his allies (Dan. 11:44). However, before he will be able to get there, God will have destroyed the huge invading army supernaturally (Ezek. 38:17—39:20).

This destruction of Antichrist's major opponent near the middle of the seventieth week will enable him to extend his rule to worldwide proportions. With no one left to challenge his authority, he will be free to do whatever he pleases. It is at that time that his false face of benevolence will come off and his true beastly character will be displayed. He will establish his headquarters in Israel (Dan. 11:45), break his covenant with that country by forcing her to cease offering her Old Testament sacrifices (Dan. 9:27), and destroy the apostate religion (Rev. 17:16).

Having brought an end to these other forms of religion, Antichrist will erect an image of himself in the holy of holies in the Jewish Temple, declare that he is God, and demand that everyone worship him (Dan. 9:27; 11:36–37; Mt. 24:15; 2 Th. 2:4). Satan will prompt him to do this because, through the worship of Antichrist, he himself will receive worship (Rev. 13:4). Most of the people of the world will have no problem worshiping Satan's king (Rev. 13:8). As a result of the current philosophy that man is evolving toward deification, or man-godhood, the world is being conditioned for this kind of worship. Because of Antichrist's supernatural powers, it will be easy for the world to conclude that he is the ultimate product of evolution; therefore, he should be worshiped as the representative of what man is becoming—deity.

Satan will give supernatural powers to another man to enable him to be the high priest of the Antichrist cult. This man, called the false prophet (Rev. 16:13; 19:20), will develop and lead a highly organized religious system on behalf of the king (Rev. 13:11–18). With the development of this system, Antichrist will

reach the peak of his career. He will be given authority to remain
in his high position for three and one-half more years (Rev. 13:5).

The Destruction of All Testimony for God. In spite of the
intense activity of Satan, God will save many people during
the seventieth week. These people will carry on an active
witness for God and Christ in the world. One of Satan's
goals will be the total annihilation of all testimony about his
Enemy. Thus he will prompt the apostate religion,
Antichrist, and the false prophet to make war against God's
saints (Dan. 7:25; Rev. 13:7, 15; 17:6). Many believers will be
martyred for their faith (Rev. 20:4), but the witness never
will cease.

The Destruction of Israel. Since Israel's repentance will be a
major key to the establishment of God's theocratic kingdom,
Satan will continue to attempt annihilation of Israel during the
seventieth week. Realizing that his time is growing short, he
will attack the nation with extreme intensity (Rev. 12).
Antichrist will persecute the Jewish people more severely than
they have ever been persecuted (Mt. 24:15–20). Anti-Semitism
will be the worst in history. For this reason Jeremiah referred to
this period as "the time of Jacob's trouble" (Jer. 30:4–7). At the
end of the seventieth week Satan will draw all the armies of the
world to Israel (Rev. 16:13–14, 16). This will threaten the existence of Israel (Zech. 14:1–2), but God will continue to preserve
at least a remnant (Jer. 30:7).

The Gathering of the Armies. Satan's last purpose for the
seventieth week will be to gather all the armies of the world
together at Armageddon in Israel. In order to accomplish
this feat, he, Antichrist, and the false prophet will resort to
demonic activity (Rev. 16:12–16). As the seventieth week
nears its end, Satan will realize that Christ soon will come to
Israel to establish the theocratic kingdom. For this reason he
will want the military might of the whole world there to help
him wage war against the Redeemer (Ps. 2:1–3; Rev. 19:19).
This will be his last-ditch attempt to prevent the theocracy
from coming.

God's Purposes for the Seventieth Week

In His war against the kingdom of Satan, God also will have four major purposes for the seventieth week.

The Salvation of Many People. Near the beginning of the seventieth week God will save 144,000 Jewish men, seal them from harm, and send them throughout the world to preach everywhere until Christ will return (Rev. 7:2–8). As a result of their evangelistic effort, a great multitude of people from every tongue, tribe, and nation will become saved (Rev. 7:9–17).[2] To the nation of Israel God will send two special witnesses who will dress like Old Testament prophets, perform great signs, and prophesy in preparation for the coming, theocratic kingdom (Rev. 11:3–13).[3] Through their testimony many Jews will become saved, and they in turn will become witnesses (Rev. 12:17).[4] Thus God will use the seventieth week to enlarge the membership of His kingdom.

The Crushing of the Kingdom of Satan. From the fall of man to the seventieth week God has been allowing Satan to try every means possible to overthrow the kingdom of God. Although God has been preventing Satan from accomplishing his goal, He has not begun to execute the sentence of judgment upon him and his kingdom. Thus Satan has been having his day. However, once the Antichrist is revealed and Satan begins his ultimate attempt of overthrow, God finally will begin to close in upon him to crush both him and his kingdom. So God will start to have His day, and the seventieth week will begin a period of time called the Day of the Lord (2 Th. 2:1–3).

The seventieth week will be characterized by divine judgment, as God pours out His wrath upon the godless people and domain of the earthly province of Satan's kingdom (Zeph. 1:14–18). Over the course of the seven years the judgments will increase in their severity, so that the latter three and one-half years will be far worse than the former. For this reason, Jesus said that the latter half of the seventieth week would be a time of "great tribulation, such as has not been from the beginning of the world until now, no, nor ever shall be. And except those days had been shortened, no flesh would have been saved" (Mt. 24:21–22). As wave after wave of judgment comes, much of the earth's surface will be ravished, and much of Antichrist's kingdom, and huge segments of the world's population will be destroyed (Rev. 6; 8–11; 16–18). As a result, the world will learn the horrible consequences of denying the existence of its Creator.

Near the middle of the seventieth week God will direct one stage of judgment against Satan himself. Michael, the archangel, and those angels of God that are under his command will attack Satan and his angels in the heaven which is their dwelling place (Rev. 12:7). As a result of this war in the spiritual realm, Satan and his angels will be evicted from their heaven and cast down to earth in partial defeat (Rev. 12:8–9). Thus Satan and the whole of his kingdom will be confined to earth to await the final battle with Christ.

As God pours out His judgments upon Satan and his kingdom, it will become evident that He is beginning to execute His program of establishing the theocratic kingdom. Thus, in eager anticipation of that blessed, coming event, the creatures of God in heaven will cry out in great exultation:

The kingdom of the world is become the kingdom of our Lord, and of His Christ: and He shall reign for ever and ever (Rev. 11:15).

Now is come the salvation, and the power, and the kingdom of our God, and the authority of His Christ: for the accuser of our brethren is cast down, [who] accuseth them before our God day and night (Rev. 12:10).

The Gathering of the Armies. Satan will not be the only one involved in gathering all the armies of the world together in Israel at the end of the seventieth week. God will have a hand in this too (Zeph. 3:8; Zech. 14:1–2; Rev. 16:1, 12). His purpose for the gathering will be that of destroying these armies of godless men (Ps. 2:4–12; Joel 3:9–16).

The Repentance of Israel. One of God's greatest purposes for the seventieth week will be that of bringing the nation of

Israel to genuine repentance. For centuries Israel has been in a state of rebellion, refusing to repent so that the theocratic kingdom could be established. As a result, she has suffered wave after wave of persecution, as one Gentile nation after another has indulged in anti-Semitism. Thus far, however, there have been other nations to which the Jewish people could appeal for refuge and aid in their times of oppression. Now, after some 1,900 years of worldwide dispersion, they once again have a nation in their homeland (as the Scriptures implied that they would at least by the time Antichrist would be revealed).

When Antichrist will persecute the Jewish people worse than they ever have been persecuted before, there will be no nations to which they can appeal for refuge or help because of the worldwide rule of their persecutor. When the armies of the world will be gathered in their homeland at the end of the seventieth week, the Jewish people will be threatened with total annihilation (Zech. 12:2–3). God will use these fantastic pressures as His instrument for backing Israel into such a tight corner that there will be no release, no means of escape unless the nation cries out to Him to deliver her by sending His Messiah. In response to that cry, Jesus Christ will come out of heaven. When the people of Israel see the wounds of His crucifixion in His resurrected body, they will repent (change their minds from rejection to acceptance of Him as their Messiah and Savior). They will mourn the fact that their nation rejected Him as the Messiah in His First Coming (Zech. 12:10–14). In response to this repentance, God will cleanse the nation from sin (Zech. 13:1).

The Second Coming of Jesus Christ

Once the armies of the world have gathered at Armageddon and Israel has repented, Jesus Christ will come riding out of Heaven on a white horse—the sign of a victorious conqueror. With Him will be all the angelic armies of heaven. Antichrist, the kings under him, and their armies will be united in the land of

Israel to make war against Christ and His angels, but they will be overcome completely by the word and brilliant glory of the Redeemer (2 Th. 2:8; Rev. 19:11, 16, 19). Antichrist and the false prophet will be cast alive into the lake of fire, there to remain forever (Rev. 19:20). The kings and their godless armies will be killed, and the birds will feed on their flesh (Joel 3:9–16; Zeph. 3:8; Zech. 12:2–9; 14:3, 12–15; Rev. 19:17–18, 21). Thus the political and military forces of Satan's kingdom will be crushed completely.

Satan himself will be bound and cast into the abyss for the next one thousand years. This means that he will be rendered totally inoperative during the reign of Christ on this present earth. His fallen, free angels will be imprisoned in the abyss (Isa. 24:21). So he will have absolutely no influence in the world during the theocratic kingdom (Rev. 20:1–3).

Once Christ reaches earth, He will gather to Israel all the Jewish people who are yet scattered across the world (Dt. 30:1–5; Mt. 24:31). Then He will enter into judgment with them. Any rebels left in the nation will be purged out, and the saved Jews will enter the theocratic kingdom (Ezek. 20:34–38; Mal. 3:2–3, 5; Mt. 25:1–30; Rom. 11:26–27).[5]

Thus, just as God promised thoughout Scripture, redeemed Israel will live forever in the homeland God gave the Jewish people, never to be scattered from it again (Gen. 12:6–7; 13:14–18; 15:7, 18–21; 17:7–8, 19–21; 26:1–3; 28:10–13; 35:9–12; Dt. 30:1–9; Isa. 60:21; Jer. 32:37–44; Ezek. 34:22–31; 36:21–28; Joel 3:16–20; Amos 9:14–15).

After Israel is judged, Christ will gather the living Gentiles to judge them. Once again, the unsaved will be banished "into everlasting fire, prepared for the devil and his angels," but the saved Gentiles will enter the theocratic kingdom (Joel 3:1–2; Mt. 25:31–46).[6]

At the time of His Second Coming, Christ will resurrect the Old Testament saints and the seventieth-week saints who died before Christ's return (Isa. 26:19; Dan. 12:2; Rev. 20:4–5).[7] They also will enter the theocratic kingdom.

Church saints will come with Christ from heaven to earth at His Second Coming, "and so shall we ever be with the Lord" (1 Th. 4:17).

The Nature of the Theocratic Kingdom

After Christ has completed the work associated with His Second Coming, He will establish the promised, theocratic kingdom (Rev. 20:4–6). The entire world will come under the rule of Christ, who, as a man born of woman, will govern the earth for God in accordance with His divine will (Ps. 2:7–8; Zech. 14:9; Rev. 11:15). As a descendant of David, He will fulfill prophetic Scripture by ruling on David's throne as King over Israel (Isa. 9:6–7; 11:1–12; Jer. 23:5–8; 33:14–16; Lk. 1:31–33; Acts 2:29–30; Rev. 22:16). As King of kings and Lord of lords, He will rule over all the Gentile monarchs and their nations (Ps. 72:8–11; Dan. 7:13–14; Zech. 14:9; Rev. 11:15; 19:16). Thus, once again, the world will enjoy a theocratic government.

When He establishes the theocratic kingdom, Christ will begin to reverse many of the tragic consequences of man's rebellion in Eden. He will make all animals tame again (Isa. 11:6–9; 65:25); heal all diseases and deformities (Isa. 33:24; 35:5–6); eliminate hazards (Ezek. 34:25–29); increase the lifespan of man (Isa. 65:20, 22); cause a great abundance of trees and fruit (Isa. 55:13; Ezek. 47:12; Joel 2:21–22), fish (Ezek. 47:9–10), and grain and wine (Joel 2:24; Amos 9:13); control the environment for the benefit of man (Ezek. 34:26–27); heal the effects of pollution (Ezek. 47:1–12); and abolish war and injustice (Isa. 2:2–4; 9:6–7; 11:2–5; Jer. 23:5; Mic. 4:1–3; Zech. 9:9–10). All these changes will constitute what Christ and Peter called "the regeneration," the "seasons of refreshing," and "the times of restoration of all things" (Mt. 19:28; Acts 3:19–21). Truly, this will be the present earth's golden age.

During the theocratic kingdom, Israel finally will fulfill the role that God originally intended for her—to be the spiritual leader of the whole world (Ex. 19:5–6). Israel's capital city, Jerusalem, will be the spiritual and political center of the world. All the nations will come there to worship Christ and be instructed according to His ways and the Word of God (Isa. 2:1–4; 11:10–12; Mic. 4:1–3).

Gentiles will call the people of Israel "the priests of the LORD" and "the ministers of our God" (Isa. 61:6). In their desire to seek the Lord in Jerusalem and to pray before Him, people from "all languages of the nations" will take hold of "a Jew, saying, We will go with you; for we have heard that God is with you" (Zech. 8:20–23). Every year all the nations will come to Jerusalem to worship Christ the King and to keep the Feast of Tabernacles (Zech. 14:16–19).

Because God has determined that Israel be the spiritual leader of the whole world during the future theocratic kingdom, He will not establish that kingdom until that nation itself is spiritually right with Him through repentance. For that reason Jesus Christ commissioned His apostles to preach the gospel of the kingdom, "Repent: for the kingdom of heaven is at hand," exclusively to the people of Israel (Mt. 10:5–7). It is Israel, not the Gentiles or Samaritans, that must be spiritually right with God before He will establish the kingdom. Thus, in accord, with God's sovereignance plan for the world, Israel remains a key to the fulfillment of God's purpose for history.

The saints of all previous ages of history will constitute the total population of the theocratic kingdom in its beginning. No unsaved people will enter the kingdom from the seventieth week. As time progresses, however, those saints who survived the seventieth week alive and entered the kingdom with mortal bodies, will give birth to unregenerate children (Jer. 30:19–20; Ezek. 47:22). No doubt many of these children will become saved as they grow up, but many others will reject Christ throughout their lives. This rejection will take place in spite of the glorious presence of Christ, the near-perfect conditions of the world, and the total absence of Satan's influence. Thus these people will demonstrate that, since the Fall, human rebellion against God really has not been the result of Satan's influence, bad world conditions, or the invisibility of God. Instead, it has been the result of man's own, sinful nature.

These unsaved will chafe under the iron-hand rule of Christ. They will be irritated by the absolute justice and inflexible righteousness that He will enforce incessantly throughout the whole world (Isa. 11:3–5; 9:7).[8] Any who rebel outwardly or sin blatantly in the open will be punished immediately with physical death

(Ps. 72:1–4; Isa. 11:4; 29:20–21; Jer. 31:29–30).[9] Rather than suffer death, many will hide their rebellion inwardly, hoping for an opportunity to overthrow Christ's reign.

The theocratic kingdom will last for 1,000 years on this present earth (Rev. 19:4–6). For this reason, many Bible scholars have called it the Millennial Kingdom and its period of time the Millennium.

Satan's Final Attempt

As Satan remains bound in the abyss for 1,000 years, he will have plenty of time to think over all the mistakes he made in his war against the kingdom of God. Having learned much about God's strategy through his defeat, he will reflect on what he could have done better to overcome that strategy. Through time he will deceive himself into thinking that, if only he could have one more chance, he could beat the sovereignty of God.

In order to demonstrate that there is absolutely no way in which His sovereign rule can be overthrown, God will afford Satan the opportunity to try his best-laid plan. Satan will be set free from the abyss for a brief period of time after the 1,000 years of the theocratic kingdom have ended (Rev. 20:3, 7). Through deception he will gather together all the malcontents of the kingdom who have been hiding their hatred of Christ's righteous reign inwardly (Rev. 20:8). As they begin to make war against the saints, God will crush this revolution immediately by destroying them with fire from heaven (Rev. 20:9). This time Satan will be cast into the lake of fire to be tormented with Antichrist and the false prophet forever (Rev. 20:10). No doubt all of Satan's angels will be cast in with him.[10] This will be his final defeat. Never again will he challenge the sovereignty of God.

The Judgment of the Unsaved

After Satan's final defeat, all the human members of his kingdom from all periods of history will be resurrected from the dead to appear before God's great, white throne of judgment. Since all of these are unsaved, the purpose of this judgment will be to determine their degree of eternal punishment, not the fact of their lost condition.[11] Once this judgment is completed, all the unsaved will be cast forever into the lake of fire to suffer eternal torment (Rev. 20:11–15). Thus Satan's entire kingdom will remain in conscious judgment, totally separated from God for all eternity.

The Destruction of Death the Heavens, and Earth

Before God brings the history of the world to a close by destroying the present heavens and earth, He will abolish death (Rev. 20:14). Because death is to be the last enemy of man abolished, this act of God will be the sign that all the tragic consequences of man's rebellion have been reversed completely through the work of Jesus Christ (1 Cor. 15:24–26). Having crushed Satan and his kingdom forever, having established His own theocratic kingdom on earth, and having reversed the tragic consequences of man's rebellion, God thereby will have demonstrated that He alone is the sovereign God.

With His purpose for the history of this present world accomplished, God will destroy the present heavens and earth, which are stained with their record of rebellion, and will create new heavens and a new earth to replace them (2 Pet. 3:10–13; Rev. 21:1).

The Nature of the Future Eternal State

All the angelic and human members of the kingdom of God will inhabit the new heavens and new earth in eternity future. They will enjoy the glorious presence and fellowship of God and Christ, together with other unspeakable blessings, forever. One great blessing will be the total absence of sin, death, pain, and sorrow (Rev. 21—22). Never again will there be a rebellion against God and His kingdom.

Conclusion

Two Interesting Questions

THE BIBLICAL PHILOSOPHY OF HISTORY poses at least two questions. The first is this: in light of all the pain and suffering involved in the consequences of rebellion, why did God create His personal subjects with a potential for rebellion? This is another way of asking why God made angels and men with wills of their own and the ability to choose between obedience and rebellion.

The Bible does not answer this question. It would seem reasonable to assume, however, that God desired to enjoy fellowship with and receive love and worship from His creatures (Gen. 3:8–9). Genuine fellowship, love, and worship are not forced or mechanical; they must be given voluntarily. Only persons who have wills of their own and the ability to choose are able to offer such things voluntarily. Evidently God decided that voluntary response, even though it involved the risk of rebellion, was worth more than a programmed, mechanical response that would guarantee no rebellion.

The second question is, Why does God let the rebellion go on so long? Why couldn't He have demonstrated His sovereignty by crushing Satan as soon as he rebelled? Again, the Bible does not give an answer. Perhaps if God had destroyed Satan immediately, other creatures later on would have concluded that the only reason for Satan's failure was that he didn't try the right method, or that he didn't have enough time to execute his plan fully. So others, thinking that they could do better, might be tempted to try their hand at overthrowing the rule of God, and the kingdom of God would experience one rebellion after another. In order to avoid any further rebellions, God gives Satan full time to try every means of overthrow possible. Through this painful object lesson, He teaches all His creatures an indelible lesson—that no one, no matter how long, how hard, or what methods he tries, can ever overthrow the sovereign rule of God. All attempts can do nothing except bring agony and defeat.

Answers to Man's Basic Questions

The biblical philosophy of history provides answers to man's three basic questions, "Where have we come from? Why are we here? Where are we going?"

In response to the question concerning where we have come from, the Bible answers that we were created by the sovereign, omnipotent God. Second, the Bible tells us we are here to know God personally and serve Him actively as members and witnesses of His universal kingdom.

The biblical answer to the third question is twofold. First, as a world and a race, we are headed for the ultimate defeat of Satan and his kingdom and the glorious victory of God and His kingdom. Second, as individuals, we are headed either for eternal blessing or eternal punishment, depending upon which kingdom we belong to. All of us were born into this world as members of the kingdom of Satan, which has a sentence of divine judgment waiting to be executed against it. But because Jesus Christ paid the full penalty for our sin, our membership can be transferred to the kingdom of God, and all judgment can be removed from us if we will trust Him personally to be our Saviour (Rom. 8:1; Col. 1:13–14). Since the rule of God, the sovereign King and Judge, cannot be overthrown, a person would be foolish indeed to "neglect so great salvation" (Ps. 2:10–12; Heb. 2:1–3).

NOTES ON SOURCES

Chapter 1: The Setting for the Conflict
[1] "Theocracy," *The Oxford English Dictionary*, 1961, Vol. XI.
[2] W. E. Vine, *An Expository Dictionary of New Testament Words*, p. 320.

*Chapter 2: From the First Human Birth
Through the Wilderness Wanderings*
[1] H. C. Leupold, *Exposition of Genesis*, p. 226.
[2] Ibid., p. 328.
[3] Samuel J. Schultz, *The Old Testament Speaks*, p. 17.
[4] Leupold, *Genesis*, p. 413.
[5] C. H. Mackintosh, *Notes on the Book of Exodus*, old. ed. p. 126; new ed. *Genesis to Deuteronomy*, p. 183.
[6] John C. Whitcomb, Jr., "The Millennial Temple of Ezekiel 40—48," p. 6.
[7] Schultz, p. 84.

Chapter 3: From the Conquest of Canaan Through the Fall of Judah
[1] John J. Davis, *Conquest and Crisis*, p. 19.
[2] Ibid., p. 40.
[3] Ibid., p. 77.
[4] Ibid., p. 97.
[5] Charles C. Ryrie, *The Basis of the Premillennial Faith*, p. 77.
[6] Ibid., p. 81.
[7] Ibid., pp. 80–81.
[8] Samuel J. Schultz, *The Old Testament Speaks*, p. 139.
[9] John J. Davis, *The Birth of a Kingdom*, p. 189.
[10] Schultz, pp.198–199.
[11] Ibid., p. 199.
[12] Ibid., p. 154.
[13] Ibid., p. 201.
[14] Ibid., p. 214.
[15] Ibid., p. 167.
[16] Ibid., p. 225.
[17] Ibid., p. 226.

¹⁸ Ibid., p. 228.
¹⁹ Ibid., p. 154.

*Chapter 4: From the Babylonian Captivity
Through the Ascension of Christ*
¹ A. T. Olmstead, *History of the Persian Empire*, p. 50.
² John C. Whitcomb, Jr., Unpublished class notes.
³ Samuel J. Schultz, *The Old Testament Speaks*, p. 412.
⁴ Charles F. Pfeiffer, *Exile and Return*, p. 119.
⁵ Whitcomb.
⁶ Norman H. Snaith, *The Jews From Cyrus To Herod*, p. 21.
⁷ Ibid., p. 22.
⁸ Charles F. Pfeiffer, *An Outline of Old Testament History*, p. 141.
⁹ Snaith, p. 23.
¹⁰ Ibid.
¹¹ Ibid., pp.22, 25–29.
¹² Ibid., p. 29.
¹³ Ibid., p. 30.
¹⁴ Ibid., pp. 35, 37.
¹⁵ Ibid., p. 37.
¹⁶ Pfeiffer, *Outline*, p. 143.
¹⁷ Snaith, p. 37.
¹⁸ Ibid.
¹⁹ Pfeiffer, *Outline*, p. 145.
²⁰ Snaith, pp. 37–39.
²¹ Pfeiffer, *Outline*, p. 145.
²² Ibid., p. 146.
²³ Snaith, p. 54.
²⁴ Merrill C. Tenney, *New Testament Times*, p. 142.

*Chapter 5: From the Removal of Israel
from the Place of Blessing Through the Reformation*
¹ John Foxe, *Foxe's Book of Martyrs*, p. 17.
² Earle E. Cairns, *Christianity Through the Centuries*, p. 98.
³ Foxe, p. 19.
⁴ Ibid., pp. 17–18.

[5] Cairns, p. 98.

[6] Ibid.

[7] Ibid., p. 100.

[8] Ibid.

[9] Ibid., p. xxii.

[10] Ibid., p. 101.

[11] Ibid.

[12] Jesse Lyman Hurlbut, *The Story of the Christian Church*, p. 73.

[13] Cairns, p. 135.

[14] Hurlbut, p. 79.

[15] Ibid.

[16] Ibid., p. 80.

[17] Ibid.

[18] Cairns, pp. 109, 122.

[19] Ibid., p. 80.

[20] Hurlbut, p. 159.

[21] Ibid., p. 160.

[22] Adolf Harnack, "Millennium," *Encyclopaedia Britannica*, 1946 ed., Vol. XV, p. 496.

[23] John F. Walvoord, *The Millennial Kingdom*, p. 44.

[24] Ibid., p. 45.

[25] Adolf Harnack, "Millennium," *Encyclopaedia Britannica*, ninth ed., Vol. XVI, p. 316.

[26] Harnack, "Millennium," *Encyclopaedia Britannica*, 1946 ed., Vol. XV, p. 496.

[27] Ibid.

[28] Walvoord, pp. 47–48.

[29] Ibid., pp. 50–51.

[30] Cairns, p. 161.

[31] Walvoord, p. 50.

[32] Ibid., p. 45.

[33] Ibid., p. 51.

[34] Cairns, p. 161.

[35] For an excellent account of the development of Replacement Theology in early Christendom, read *Israel in the Development of Christian Thought* by Ronald E. Diprose (Rome: Istituto

Evangelico Italiano, 2000).
[36] Hurlbut, pp. 130–131.
[37] Ibid., p. 115.
[38] Ibid., p. 116.
[39] Ibid., p. 117.
[40] Ibid.
[41] Harnack, "Millennium," *Encyclopaedia Britannica*, 1946 ed., p. 497.
[42] For an account of such groups, see E. H. Broadbent, *The Pilgrim Church*, 1963.
[43] Hurlbut, pp. 142–143.
[44] Ibid., p. 143.
[45] Ibid., pp. 142–143.
[46] Cairns, p. 283.
[47] Ibid., p. 284.
[48] Hurlbut, p. 150.
[49] Cairns, p. 287.
[50] Hurlbut, pp. 150–151.
[51] Cairns, p. 287.
[52] Hurlbut, p. 151.
[53] Ibid., pp.151–154.
[54] Ibid., pp. 155–156.
[55] Cairns, pp. 331–333.
[56] Hurlbut, p. 156.
[57] Cairns, pp. 341–343.
[58] Ibid., pp. 349–353, 333–334.
[59] Ibid., pp. 344–348.
[60] Ibid., pp. 354–362.
[61] Ibid., pp. 385–386.

*Chapter 6: From the Counter Reformation
Through the Philosophy of Ritschl*
[1] Earle E. Cairns, *Christianity Through the Centuries*, pp. 379–380.
[2] Ibid., pp. 377–378.
[3] Ibid, p. 378.
[4] Ibid., pp. 376–378, 350.

[5] Ibid., p. 343.

[6] Ibid., p. 360.

[7] Ibid., pp. 361–362.

[8] Louis B. Wright, "The World of Elizabeth I," p. 673.

[9] Cairns, p. 362.

[10] Ibid., p. 351.

[11] Ibid., pp. 380–382.

[12] Ibid., p. 338.

[13] Ibid., pp. 331–334.

[14] Ibid., pp. 332–333.

[15] Ibid., p. 405.

[16] Ibid., p. 407.

[17] Ibid., pp. 407–408.

[18] Ibid., pp. 408, 410.

[19] Ibid., p. 409.

[20] Ibid.

[21] Ibid., p. 411.

[22] Ibid.

[23] Ibid., pp. 412–414.

[24] Ibid., pp. 416–419.

[25] Ibid., p. 401.

[26] John Dillenberger and Claude Welch, *Protestant Christianity*, p. 157.

[27] Ibid., p. 158.

[28] Ibid., p. 181.

[29] Ibid., p. 197.

[30] Ibid., p. 188.

[31] Ibid.

[32] Ibid., p. 197.

[33] Ibid., p. 189.

[34] Ibid., p. 195.

[35] Cairns, p. 447.

[36] Dillenberger and Welch, p. 195.

[37] Ibid., p. 189.

[38] Ibid., p. 194.

[39] Ibid., p. 195.

[40] Ibid.
[41] Donald Grey Barnhouse, *The Invisible War,* p. 66.
[42] Cairns, pp. 449–450.
[43] Dillenberger and Welch, p. 239.
[44] Ibid., p. 240.
[45] Cairns, p. 452.
[46] Dillenberger and Welch, p. 239.
[47] Ibid., p. 241.
[48] Ibid., pp. 201–202.
[49] Ibid., p. 202.
[50] Ibid.
[51] Cairns, p. 450.
[52] Ibid., p. 451.
[53] Dillenberger and Welch, p. 206.
[54] Cairns, p. 451.
[55] Dillenberger and Welch, p. 206.
[56] Cairns, p. 451.
[57] Dillenberger and Welch, p. 202.
[58] Ibid.
[59] G. G. Simpson, *The Meaning of Evolution,* p. 344.
[60] Dillenberger and Welch, pp. 205–206.
[61] Cairns, p. 451.
[62] Ibid., pp. 439, 456.
[63] Ibid., pp. 454–456.
[64] Ibid., p. 456.
[65] Ibid., p. 457.
[66] Dillenberger and Welch, p. 199.
[67] Ibid., p. 200.
[68] Ibid.
[69] Ibid., p. 199.
[70] Ibid., p. 222.
[71] Ibid., p. 200.

*Chapter 7: From Liberal Protestantism
Through the Denial of a Personal God*
[1] John Dillenberger and Claude Welch, *Protestant Christianity,* p. 207.

[2] Ibid., p. 211.

[3] Ibid., p. 225.

[4] Ibid., pp. 212–213.

[5] Ibid., p. 213.

[6] Ibid.

[7] Ibid., pp. 213–214.

[8] Ibid., p. 214.

[9] Ibid., p. 215.

[10] Ibid.

[11] Ibid., p. 216.

[12] Ibid., p. 217.

[13] Ibid., pp. 217–218.

[14] Ibid., p. 218.

[15] Ibid., pp. 219, 222.

[16] Ibid., pp. 219–220.

[17] Ibid., pp. 218, 222.

[18] Ibid., p. 219.

[19] Ibid., pp.219–222.

[20] Earle E. Cairns, *Christianity Through the Centuries*, p. 464.

[21] Dillenberger and Welch, p. 223.

[22] Ibid., p. 243.

[23] Ibid., p. 244.

[24] Ibid., p. 232.

[25] Cairns, p. 463.

[26] Ibid.

[27] Dillenberger and Welch, pp. 232, 246.

[28] Ibid., p. 252.

[29] Ibid.

[30] Cairns, p. 481.

[31] Ibid.

[32] Ibid.

[33] Ibid., p. 480.

[34] Dillenberger and Welch, p. 291.

[35] Ibid., p. 292.

[36] Ibid.

[37] Ibid., p. 294.

[38] Ibid., p. 295.

[39] Ibid., pp. 253, 290.

[40] Ibid., p. 253.

[41] Ibid., p. 258.

[42] Ibid.

[43] Ibid., pp. 264–266.

[44] Ibid., pp. 269–273.

[45] Ibid., pp. 277–278.

[46] Ibid., p. 279.

[47] Ibid., p. 274.

[48] Ibid., p. 281.

[49] Ibid., p. 274.

[50] Ibid., p. 276.

[51] Ibid.

[52] Ibid., p. 279.

[53] Ibid., pp. 282–283.

[54] Ibid., p. 258.

[55] Ibid., p. 259.

[56] John Charles Cooper, *The Roots of the Radical Theology*, pp. 118, 121.

[57] Ibid., p. 135.

[58] Harold O. J. Brown, "Dreams of a Third Age," *Christianity Today*, XV, 21 (July 16, 1971), 4 [952].

[59] William E. Hordern, *A Layman's Guide to Protestant Theology*, pp. 170, 182, 184.

[60] Gerd Ludemann, *The Great Deception: And What Jesus Really Said and Did*, p. 8.

[61] *Humanist Manifesto II*, American Humanist Association, [www.humanist.net/documents/manifesto2.html], pp. 2–3.

Chapter 8: From Human Despair
Through the Move Toward Globalism
[1] John Charles Cooper, *The Roots of Radical Theology*, p. 141.

[2] *Humanist Manifesto II*. American Humanist Association, [www.humanist.net/documents/manifesto2.html], p. 3.

[3] Harold O. J. Brown, "Dreams of a Third Age," *Christianity*

Today, XV, 21 (July 16, 1971), 4 [952].

[4] Ibid.

[5] John Leo, "On Society—Notes of a nonvictim," *U.S. News & World Report* (October 6, 1997), p. 11.

[6] Neil Postman & Charles Weingartner, *Teaching as a Subversive Activity*, pp. 98–99.

[7] Ibid., pp. 216–217.

[8] Quoted by "The Buzz: Q & A with 'God,'" *World*, (May 11, 2002), p. 7.

[9] John Leo, "On Society—A no-fault Holocaust," *U.S. News & World Report* (July 21, 1997), p. 14.

[10] Quoted by Gertrude Himmelfarb, *Darwin and the Darwinian Revolution*, p. 386.

[11] Quoted by John Leo, "On Society—An outing is no picnic," *U.S. News & World Report* (May 22, 2000), p. 20.

[12] Midge Decter, "The Assault on the Boy Scouts of America," *IMPRIMIS*, Vol. 31, No. 5 (May 2002), pp. 2, 5–6. Reprinted by permission from IMPRIMIS, the national speech digest of Hillsdale College [www.hillsdale.edu].

[13] Ibid., p. 5.

[14] Ibid., p. 2.

[15] Ibid., p. 4.

[16] Ibid., p. 6.

[17] John Leo, "On Society—No takeovers, please," *U.S. News & World Report* (January 19, 1998), p. 13.

[18] John Leo, "On Society—A Kinder, Gentler Army," *U.S. News & World Report* (August 11, 1997), p. 14.

[19] Ibid.

[20] Ibid.

[21] Quoted by John Leo, "On Society—Mars to Venus: Back off," *U.S. News & World Report* (May 11, 1998), p. 16.

[22] John Leo, "Mars to Venus," p. 16.

[23] Ibid.

[24] Lionel Tiger, "Nasty turns in family life," *U.S. News & World Report* (July 1, 1996), p. 57.

[25] Ibid.

[26] Ibid.

[27] Ibid.

[28] Ibid.

[29] Ibid.

[30] Leo, "Mars to Venus."

[31] Recounted and quoted by John Leo, "Mars to Venus."

[32] Quoted by Marvin Olasky, "Let boys be boys," World (August 18, 2001), p.38.

[33] Ibid.

[34] Ibid.

[35] Ibid.

[36] Ibid.

[37] Kenneth L. Woodward, "Feminism and the Churches," Newsweek (February 13, 1989), p. 58.

[38] Ibid., p. 59.

[39] Ibid., p. 58.

[40] Ibid., pp. 58, 60–61.

[41] Ibid., pp. 59–60.

[42] Quoted by Kenneth L. Woodward, Ibid., p. 60.

[43] Michael S. McManus, "Presbyterians outraged by 'Re-Imagining' conference," March 19, 1994.

[44] Ibid.

[45] Woodward, "Feminism and the Churches," p. 61.

[46] Humanist Manifesto II, p. 3.

[47] Cooper, p. 155.

[48] Dillenberger and Welch, p. 290.

[49] Cooper, p.155.

[50] Humanist Manifesto II, p. 6.

[51] Ibid., p. 7.

[52] United Nations Press Release GA 9758, September 8, 2000: "World Leaders Adopt 'United Nations Millenium Declaration' at Conclusion of Extraordinary Three Day Summit," [http://www0.un.org/News/Press/docs/2000/20000908.ga9758.doc.html], home page [www.un.org].

[53] Ibid.

[54] Ibid.

55 Dillenberger and Welch, p. 290

56 Editors of *Religion Today*, "Current News Summary" (October 19, 1999), [www.religiontoday.crosswalk.com/CurrentNewsSummary], home page [www.crosswalk.com].

57 Ibid., May 23, 2000.

58 Ibid., July 11, 2000.

59 Ibid., July 11, 2000.

60 James Harder, "U.N. Faithful Eye Global Religion," *Insight Magazine* (October 2, 2000), [www.insightmag.com/archive/200010034.shtml], home page [www.insightmag.com].

61 Quoted by James Harder, Ibid.

62 Ibid.

63 James Harder, "U.N. Faithful."

64 Quoted by James Harder, Ibid.

65 James Harder, "U.N. Faithful."

66 Quoted by James Harder, Ibid.

67 Quoted by Jeffrey L. Sheler, "Pull back or reach out?," *U.S. News & World Report* (September 18, 2000), p. 74.

68 Ibid.

69 Editors of *Religion Today*, "Current News Summary" (September 18, 2000), [www.religiontoday.crosswalk.com/Current NewsSummary], home page [www.crosswalk.com].

70 Ibid., September 7, 2000.

71 Quoted by Jeffrey L. Sheler, "Plotting world order in Rome," *U.S. News & World Report* (June 10, 1996), p. 66.

72 Joel Belz, "The other fundamentalists," *World* (May/June, 2002), p. 5.

73 Ibid.

74 Ibid.

75 Gene Edward Veith, "Christians as Taliban," *World* (January 19, 2002), p. 14.

76 Ibid.

78 Norman Geisler, "What New Agers Believe," *Word of Life Quarterly* (Winter, 1991), p. 12.

79 Cooper, p. 117.

[80] Ibid., p. 148.
[81] Quoted by Brown, "Dreams," Ibid.
[82] Cooper, 156–157.
[83] Ibid., p. 154.
[84] Ibid., pp. 154–155.
[85] Ibid., p. 155.
[86] Ibid., p. 156.
[87] Norman Geisler, "What New Agers Believe," Ibid.
[88] Ibid.

Chapter 9: From the Rapture of the Church to Eternity Future
[1] J. Dwight Pentecost, *Things to Come*, pp. 204–205, 259–263.
[2] Ibid., p. 300.
[3] Ibid., pp. 211–212.
[4] Ibid., pp. 295, 297.
[5] Ibid., pp.413–415.
[6] Ibid., pp. 415–422.
[7] Ibid., p. 411.
[8] Ibid., p. 503.
[9] Ibid.
[10] Ibid., pp. 422–423.
[11] Ibid., p. 424.

SELECTED BIBLIOGRAPHY

Books

Barnhouse, Donald Grey. *The Invisible War.* Grand Rapids: Zondervan, 1965.

Broadbent, E. H. *The Pilgrim Church.* London: Pickering & Inglis Ltd., 1963.

Cairns, Earle E. *Christianity Through the Centuries.* Grand Rapids: Zondervan, 1964.

Cooper, John Charles. *The Roots of the Radical Theology.* Philadelphia: Westminster, 1967.

Davis, John J. *Conquest and Crisis.* Grand Rapids: Baker, 1969.

—————. *The Birth of a Kingdom.* Winona Lake, Ind.: B M H Books, 1970.

Dillenberger, John, and Claude Welch. *Protestant Christianity.* New York: Scribner, 1954.

Foxe, John. *Foxe's Book of Martyrs.* Philadelphia: publisher's name missing, n.d.

Himmelfarb, Gertrude. *Darwin and the Darwinian Revolution.* New York: Norton, 1968.

Hordern, William E. *A Layman's Guide to Protestant Theology,* rev. ed. New York: The Macmillan Company, 1972.

Hurlbut, Jesse Lyman. *The Story of the Christian Church.* Philadelphia: Winston, 1933.

Leupold, H. C. *Exposition of Genesis.* Columbus, Ohio: Wartburg, 1942.

Ludemann, Gerd. *The Great Deception: And What Jesus Really Said and Did.* Amherst: Prometheus Books, 1999.

Mackintosh, C. H. *Notes on the Pentateuch (Exodus).* Neptune, New Jersey: Loizeaux Brothers, 6 vols. 1880; 1–vol. ed. *Genesis to Deuteronomy: Notes on the Pentateuch,* 1973.

Olmstead, A. T. *History of the Persian Empire.* Chicago: University of Chicago, 1959.

Pentecost, J. Dwight. *Things to Come.* Grand Rapids: Dunham, 1959.

Pfeiffer, Charles F. *An Outline of Old Testament History.* Chicago: Moody Press, 1960.

————. *Exile and Return*. Grand Rapids: Baker, 1962.

Postman, Neil, and Weingartner, Charles. *Teaching as a Subversive Activity*. New York: Dell Publishing Co., 1969.

Ryrie, Charles C. *The Basis of the Premillennial Faith*. Neptune, New Jersey: Loizeaux Brothers, 1953.

Schultz, Samuel J. *The Old Testament Speaks*. New York: Harper, 1960.

Simpson, G. G. *The Meaning of Evolution*. New Haven: Yale University, 1949.

Snaith, Norman H. *The Jews From Cyrus to Herod*. Nashville: Abingdon, n.d.

Tenney, Merrill C. *New Testament Times*. Grand Rapids: Eerdmans, 1965.

Vine, W. E. *An Expository Dictionary of New Testament Words*. Westwood, New Jersey: Revell, 1959.

Walvoord, John F. *The Millennial Kingdom*. Findlay, Ohio: Dunham, 1959.

Articles

Belz, Joel. "The other fundamentalists." *WORLD*, May/June, 2002, p. 5.

Brown, Harold O. J. "Dreams of a Third Age." *Christianity Today*, XV, 21, July 16, 1971, 4 [952].

Decter, Midge. "The Assault on the Boy Scouts of America." *IMPRIMIS*, publication of Hillsdale College, Vol. 31, No. 5, May 2002, pp. 2, 5–6.

Editors of *Religion Today*, "Current News Summary." October 19, 1999, [www.religiontoday.crosswalk.com/ CurrentNewsSummary], home page [www.crosswalk.com].

Geisler, Norman. "What New Agers Believe." *Word of Life Quarterly*, Winter, 1991, p. 12.

Harder, James. "U.N. Faithful Eye Global Religion." *Insight Magazine*, October 2, 2000, [www.insightmag.com/ archive/200010034.shtml], home page [www.insightmag.com].

Harnack, Adolf. "Millennium." *Encyclopaedia Britannica*. Ninth ed., Vol. XVI.

Harnack, Adolf. "Millennium." *Encyclopaedia Britannica.* 1946 ed. Vol. XV.

Humanist Manifesto II. American Humanist Association. 1973.

Leo, John. "On Society—Notes of a nonvictim." *U.S. News & World Report,* October 6, 1997, p. 11.

———. "On Society—A no-fault Holocaust." *U.S. News & World Report,* July 21, 1997, p. 14.

———. "On Society—An outing is no picnic." *U.S. News & World Report,* May 22, 2000, p. 20.

———. "On Society—No takeovers, please." *U.S. News & World Report,* January 19, 1998, p. 13.

———. "On Society—A kinder, gentler Army." *U.S. News & World Report,* August 11, 1997, p. 14.

———. "On Society—Mars to Venus: Back off." *U.S. News & World Report,* May 11, 1998, p. 16.

McManus, Michael S., "Presbyterians outraged by 'Re-Imagining' conference." March 19, 1994.

Olasky, Marvin. "Let boys be boys." *World,* August 18, 2001, p. 38.

Sheler, Jeffrey L. "Plotting world order in Rome." *U.S. News & World Report,* June 10, 1996, p. 66.

———. "Pull back or reach out?" *U. S. News & World Report,* September 18, 2000, p. 74.

"The Buzz: Q & A with 'God.'" *World,* May 11, 2002, p. 7.

"Theocracy." *The Oxford English Dictionary.* 1961, vol. XI.

Tiger, Lionel. "Nasty turns in family life." *U.S. News & World Report,* July 1, 1996, p. 57.

United Nations Press Release GA 9758. "World Leaders Adopt 'United Nations Millenium Declaration' at Conclusion of Extraordinary Three Day Summit," September 8, 2000, [www0.un.org/News/Press/docs/2000/20000908.ga9758.doc.html], home page [www.un.org].

Veith, Gene Edward. "Christians as Taliban." *World,* January 19, 2002, p. 14.

Woodward, Kenneth L. "Feminism and the Churches."

Newsweek, February 13, 1989, p. 58.

Wright, Louis B. "The World of Elizabeth l." *National Geographic,* November 1968, p.673.

Unpublished Materials

Whitcomb, John C., Jr. "The Millennial Temple of Ezekiel 40—48." Unpublished paper presented to class entitled, "Old Testament Major Prophets," Grace Theological Seminary, n.d.

————. "Exile and Restoration." Unpublished class notes, Grace Theological Seminary, 1969.

More Books by
Renald E. Showers

MARANATHA: OUR LORD, COME!
A Definitive Study of the Rapture of the Church
This in-depth study addresses such issues as the Day of the Lord, its relationship to the Time of Jacob's Trouble and the Great Tribulation, the 70 Weeks of Daniel, and much more. Learn why the timing of the Rapture has practical implications for daily living and ministry.
ISBN 0-915540-22-3, #B55P

THERE REALLY IS A DIFFERENCE
A Comparison of Covenant and Dispensational Theology
Learn how theological differences affect such issues as God's ultimate purpose for history, God's program for Israel, the church, and the Christian's relationship to the Mosaic Law and grace. This excellent book also explores the differences between the premillennial, amillennial, and postmillennial views of the Kingdom of God and presents an apology for the dispensational-premillennial system of theology.
ISBN 0-915540-50-9, #B36

THE MOST HIGH GOD

One of the finest commentaries on the book of Daniel available today, this clear, concise, and consistently premillennial exposition sheds tremendous light on prophecy, the Times of the Gentiles, and other portions of the prophetic Word.
ISBN 0-915540-30-4, #B26

TWO MILLENNIA OF CHURCH HISTORY

This comprehensive, easy-to-understand, and beautifully illustrated 24-page booklet puts 2,000 years of church history at your fingertips. An exceptional resource, it will enable you to trace the development of first-century Orthodoxy, Romanism, the Reformation, liberal theology, the great spiritual awakenings, and much, much more.
ISBN 0-915540-67-3, #B82

THE FOUNDATIONS OF FAITH
Volume 1

This is a compiliation of Dr. Showers' in-depth studies in systematic theology. *The Revealed and Personal Word of God* is the first in the series and covers bibliology and Chrisology—the doctrines of the Bible and the Messiah. This hardback, fully indexed volume is a must for any serious student of God's Word.
ISBN 0-915540-77-0, #B89

For current prices, to order by credit card, or to obtain a complete catalog of all the resources available from The Friends of Israel, call us at **800-345-8461**; visit our Web store at **www.foi.org**; or write us at **P.O. Box 908, Bellmawr, NJ 08099.**